Faithful

Meditations

for
Every Day in
Ordinary Time

———⟆———

Weeks 11–22

YEARS A, B, & C

Faithful

Meditations

for
Every Day in
Ordinary Time

— ⟆ —

Weeks 11–22

Rev. Warren J. Savage
Mary Ann McSweeny

Liguori
ONE LIGUORI DRIVE
LIGUORI MO 63057-9999

Imprimi Potest:
Harry Grile, CSsR, Provincial
Denver Province, The Redemptorists

Published by Liguori Publications
Liguori, Missouri 63057

To order, call 800-325-9521
www.liguori.org

Library of Congress Cataloging-in-Publication Data
On file

Liguori Publications, a nonprofit corporation, is an apostolate of
The Redemptorists. To learn more about The Redemptorists,
visit Redemptorists.com.

Printed in the United States of America
17 16 15 14 13 / 5 4 3 2 1
First Edition

Contents

Introduction

We live in a challenging and complex world. We're confronted with human and social problems that call for reasonable and sustainable solutions. We've witnessed extraordinary advances in the fields of science and technology that have given us a greater understanding of life and the intricate dynamics of human nature.

We have more confidence in our ability to shape our way of life and control the events of the world. Many who study and research the universe and human nature have come to believe we're the masters of our own destiny. There is no longer a need and place for God.

Among the challenges facing Christian believers, proclaiming faith in God as the source and foundation of everything is one that cannot be ignored. For Christians, faith matters because God matters. Christians have a duty and obligation to preserve and share their faith.

Faith is a gift from God. It's an invitation extended to all people to live in communion with God. Faith is the response of humble men and women who recognize that the universe and life are born out of the mystery called God. The meaning and purpose of life cannot be understood apart from a relationship with God. A Christian is a person of faith who sees life from within the context of God's world revealed in the sacred Scripture and interpreted in light of the human condition.

The Christian person makes every effort to discern and live by God's will and tries to respond to the challenges and complexities of life with the wisdom of God. God sent Jesus into the world to proclaim a message of peace, love, compassion, and forgiveness to all people. This mission has been given to all Christians, who must be God's voice in a secular world.

This collection of daily Scripture readings, reflections, prayers, and practices is intended to strengthen and nurture the Christian faith. Motivated and inspired by the wisdom of God, Christians can preserve their gift of faith and remain faithful to the call to believe what they read, teach what they believe, and practice what they teach.

Eleventh Sunday in Ordinary Time

YEAR A

Exodus 19:2–6a
Psalm 100:1–2, 3, 5
Romans 5:6–11
Matthew 9:36–10:8

When [Jesus] saw the crowds, he had compassion for them, because they were harassed and helpless, like sheep without a shepherd.

MATTHEW 9:36

Reflection: Pain, suffering, brokenness, loneliness, alienation, despair, confusion, and humiliation are experiences of the human condition that move us to compassion. We don't have to look these words up to understand their meaning and impact. We see pain in the faces of people living with debilitating illnesses. We see brokenness in friends struggling with separation and divorce. We see alienation when young people turn to drugs and violence. We see despair when we encounter the poor and homeless on our streets. We witness confusion when our civic and religious leaders don't do what is right. We see people being humiliated and ridiculed for their religious beliefs, social status, racial makeup, and sexual orientation.

When Jesus saw the crowds, he could sense the collective sadness, pain, and suffering the people had endured. His immediate response was to show them the compassion of God. His next challenge was to find a way to meet the spiritual and physical needs of the people. Jesus knew that compassion alone was not enough. Compassion must always be matched with right action.

Every day we walk among crowds in the public arena, on the streets, and in the shopping malls. We must remember that every person, on some level, feels helpless and torn apart by a painful experience. Jesus teaches us that in the crowds are many who feel harassed and helpless.

No matter where we go, we must go with a shepherd's heart, ready to offer friends *and* strangers the compassion of God.

Ponder: When have I felt harassed and helpless?

Prayer: Lord, you are the compassion of God in the world. Help me be more sensitive to others' needs and concerns and to share your compassion with them.

Practice: Today I will be faithful in responding compassionately to someone in need.

YEAR B

Ezekiel 17:22–24
Psalm 92:2–3, 13–14, 15–16
2 Corinthians 5:6–10
Mark 4:26–34

[Jesus] also said, "With what can we compare the kingdom of God, or what parable will we use for it? It is like a mustard seed, which, when sown upon the ground, is the smallest of all the seeds on earth; yet when it is sown it grows up and becomes the greatest of all shrubs, and puts forth large branches, so that the birds of the air can make nests in its shade."

MARK 4:30–32

Reflection: The secular kingdom conditions us to believe that to be happy, powerful, influential, and successful, we need lots of money, the right connections, a big home, a nice car, a college degree, and a good career. People with power are attractive and draw attention from other power brokers.

Many in the secular kingdom also believe that the world's big problems can be resolved with the intervention and expertise of powerful private and public institutions.

One thing is certain about the secular kingdom: It has no room for God.

On the other hand, the kingdom of God is like

a mustard seed, small and seemingly insignificant and powerless. The power of the kingdom of God is not in its size, but in the message it proclaims: the death and resurrection of Jesus.

This simple message has the power to change the world. People conditioned by this message understand the power hidden in the seeds of love, compassion, peace, nonviolence, and forgiveness. These seeds are given to the followers of the risen Lord to be planted in the world.

People of the kingdom of God realize that the message of the risen Lord isn't always attractive and might be rejected. Those who choose to live in the kingdom of God must remain faithful to the work of planting good seeds in the hearts of all people.

Ponder: What kingdom do I live in?

Prayer: Lord, you reveal the kingdom of God to all people. Help me bear witness to God's kingdom of compassion and peace.

Practice: Today I will be faithful by performing a small act of kindness.

YEAR C

2 Samuel 12:7–10, 13
Psalm 32:1–2, 5, 7, 11
Galatians 2:16, 19–21
Luke 7:36—8:3

"Therefore, I tell you, her sins, which were many, have been forgiven; hence she has shown great love. But the one to whom little is forgiven, loves little." Then [Jesus] said to her, "Your sins are forgiven."

LUKE 7:47–48

Reflection: We feel like a sinner, an outsider, when people tell us we're not good enough. In our society, some people are made to feel like sinners because of the way they look or because they speak a foreign language, come from a different culture or social background, live a certain way, or practice a different religious tradition.

It's difficult to show great love when we haven't received it. We're not afraid to show great love when people affirm our human dignity, respect us, and recognize our innate goodness. We can embrace others more fully when people appreciate, welcome, and celebrate the richness of our culture, customs, and religious tradition. We can be more generous and compassionate when people have been kind to us.

Jesus offers all sinners the possibility of true

freedom by sharing with them the unconditional love, compassion, and forgiveness of God. When we experience God's unconditional love, we can show great love to strangers. When we experience God's compassion, we can show compassion to the poor and suffering. When we experience God's forgiveness, we can show forgiveness from the heart. Our experience of Jesus compels us to be the presence of God in a world that shows little love and forgiveness.

Ponder: What do I need to seek forgiveness for?

Prayer: Lord, your love and forgiveness bring peace to the world. Open my heart to show great love and forgiveness to all people.

Practice: Today I will be faithful by being understanding and forgiving toward a colleague.

Monday of the Eleventh Week in Ordinary Time

YEAR I
2 Corinthians 6:1–10
Psalm 98:1, 2b, 3–4

YEAR II
1 Kings 21:1–16
Psalm 5:2–3ab, 4b–6a, 6b–7

YEARS I AND II
Matthew 5:38–42

[Jesus taught them, saying,] "You have heard that it was said, 'An eye for an eye and a tooth for a tooth.' But I say to you, Do not resist an evildoer. But if anyone strikes you on the right cheek, turn the other also."

MATTHEW 5:38–39

Reflection: Jesus teaches us to have the faith to confront evil with nonviolence. When we refuse to react to violence, abuse, and cruelty with similar acts, we ground ourselves in the law of love. When we reject revenge and retaliation, we adopt the way of Jesus: the way of forgiveness, reconciliation, and compassion.

Every day, vicious acts are perpetrated. We feel powerless when nations declare war against each other. We feel victimized when adults abuse children. We feel helpless in the face of escalating anger among young people who act out in the forms of bullying, suicide, and violent assault.

Yet as we reflect on Jesus' teaching, we come to realize we are not powerless. We have the power of faith in God's loving presence. We have the power to treat everyone we meet with respect and courtesy.

We're not victims. We can't control others, but we can make choices that help promote peace, protect the vulnerable, and ensure that all people are treated with dignity and justice.

We're not helpless. We have God's Spirit to give us the courage to face the challenges of our times without losing hope. We have God's Spirit to guide us as we let go of all that prevents us from practicing peace and nonviolence. We have God's Spirit to remind us to trust in God's vision of a human family unified in love and compassion.

Ponder: How do I respond to violence?

Prayer: Lord, you show me a new way to live. Help me choose faith over distrust, love over fear, and nonviolence over aggression.

Practice: Today I will be faithful by deliberately using words of peace.

Tuesday of the Eleventh Week in Ordinary Time

YEAR I

2 Corinthians 8:1–9
Psalm 146:2, 5–6ab, 6c–7, 8–9a

YEAR II

1 Kings 21:17–29
Psalm 51:3–4, 5–6ab, 11, 16

YEARS I AND II

Matthew 5:43–48

"Be perfect, therefore, as your heavenly Father is perfect."

MATTHEW 5:48

Reflection: We become what we see and hear. We learned what it means to be a good person from our parents, neighbors, teachers, coaches, mentors, and friends. They taught us to love our brothers and sisters, to be kind and respectful toward everyone. We observed how the people in our community treated each other. We spoke and acted like the adults. We relied on them to model good behavior; we trusted them to guide us along the pathway of goodness.

We need people of faith to be seen and heard in all areas. We need people of faith to model what it means to live a spiritual life—to be like God. People of faith become the goodness of God by reading and meditating on God's Word, praying, and practicing charity. We attract others to the spiritual life when our lives reflect what is in our hearts. It's difficult to understand the spiritual life without good role models.

We know we're not perfect and that we don't live in a perfect world. People from all walks of life are starving for goodness. Our children and youth are looking for good mentors. All over the world, we hunger and thirst for strong, stable, spiritual leadership.

Deep in our hearts we know we must be better role models. We must perfect the art of being compassionate, kind, generous, loving, and forgiving toward *everyone*. We must remember that our words and actions influence people's lives. We must be perfect as God is perfect.

Ponder: What about myself must I try to perfect?

Prayer: Lord, you teach us the ways of God. May your life inspire me to be kind, compassionate, and forgiving.

Practice: Today I will be faithful by being a good role model for others.

Wednesday of the Eleventh Week in Ordinary Time

YEAR I

2 Corinthians 9:6–11
Psalm 112:1bc–2, 3–4, 9

YEAR II

2 Kings 2:1, 6–14
Psalm 31:20, 21, 24

YEARS I AND II

Matthew 6:1–6, 16–18

[Jesus taught them, saying,] "But when you give alms, do not let your left hand know what your right hand is doing, so that your alms may be done in secret; and your Father who sees in secret will reward you."

MATTHEW 6:3–4

Reflection: We're accustomed to being asked for information: name, address, cell phone number, e-mail address, what we do for a living, how many children we have, how many cars we own, what our hobbies are, how much exercise we get, how many cups of coffee we drink. Even our machines ask us for login IDs and passwords. It seems like everywhere we go our personal information is being gathered, our privacy being invaded.

Jesus calls us to guard our privacy at certain times. He tells us to give alms in secret, to pray in secret, and to fast in secret. We don't have to reveal our good deeds to anyone. Our goodness becomes self-evident the more we practice generosity, the more we deepen our knowledge of God through prayer, and the more we fast from greed, selfishness, indifference, resentment, gossip, prejudice, and dissatisfaction.

In each of us is the human need to be recognized. Yet as our faith in God's tender love for us grows, we find that our dependency on the approval of other people lessens. We have no need to divulge the good we do because it has become an integral part of who we are, a natural expression of our inner goodness and love. We learn to live from that heart space of goodness, freed from satisfying society's need to know and secure in our knowledge of God's acceptance, love, and compassion.

Ponder: In whom do I confide my acts of almsgiving, prayer, and fasting?

Prayer: Lord, you see me with eyes of love. Help me let go of my need for others' approval.

Practice: Today I will be faithful by doing a kindness for someone in secret.

Thursday of the Eleventh Week in Ordinary Time

YEAR I

2 Corinthians 11:1–11
Psalm 111:1b–2, 3–4, 7–8

YEAR II

Sirach 48:1–14
Psalm 97:1–2, 3–4, 5–6, 7

YEARS I AND II

Matthew 6:7–15

"Give us this day our daily bread."

MATTHEW 6:11

Reflection: We know what physical hunger and thirst feel like. We're fortunate because we have easy access to food and drink. When we're eating and drinking, we're not always mindful of our deeper hunger and thirst. We try to ignore that on some level we're still starving; part of us feels empty and unfulfilled. We can satisfy the needs of the body but not the soul.

We know what spiritual hunger and thirst feel like. We hunger for love, compassion, affirmation, and acceptance. We thirst for inner peace, community, a sense of belonging, friendship, and support. We struggle daily to satisfy our spiritual hunger and thirst. When we experience spiritual anguish, we don't fully realize that we really hunger and thirst for communion with God. God satisfies the spiritual longings of our hearts. Without communion with God, we have no life, hope, or peace.

People of faith must always be mindful of our spiritual longings and our dependency on God. Each day, we must reorient our lives toward God. We must remember that we can access God through prayer and that we feed our spiritual life with the food of the Scriptures and the food of the Eucharist. God satisfies our hungry hearts and souls. We're called to share what we have with others.

Ponder: How would I describe and satisfy my spiritual hunger and thirst?

Prayer: Lord, you are the bread of life for the world. Help me be your bread of love, compassion, and peace.

Practice: Today I will be faithful by praying the Our Father for greater peace and love.

Friday of the Eleventh Week in Ordinary Time

YEAR I
2 Corinthians 11:18, 21–30
Psalm 34:2–3, 4–5, 6–7

YEAR II
2 Kings 11:1–4, 9–18, 20
Psalm 132:11, 12, 13–14, 17–18

YEARS I AND II
Matthew 6:19–23

[Jesus taught them, saying,] "For where your treasure is, there your heart will be also."

MATTHEW 6:21

Reflection: Faith is a treasure that holds us steady in times of sadness, difficulty, or distress. Faith reassures us that God is always with us—loving us, guiding us, comforting us. Faith encourages us to trust in God's love. Faith calls us to put our lives and wills into God's loving care.

Faith impels us to ask for help when life's burdens are too much to bear. Faith teaches us the power of the community to heal and renew. Faith shows us our need for love and companionship.

Faith leads us to deepen our relationship with God through prayer and meditation. Faith drives our desire for conscious contact with God. Faith is what looks for God and what finds God.

Faith guides our study of sacred Scripture so that we become more intimate with God's Word. Faith gives us Jesus as our example of compassion, forgiveness, and service. Faith translates our study of Scripture into concrete actions of love, peace, and generosity.

Faith supports our intimate connection to the Spirit within us. Faith gives us the courage to follow where the Spirit leads, even when it doesn't seem to make sense. Faith bears witness to the Spirit's joyful and loving energy.

Faith opens our eyes to see God's face in others. Faith opens our ears to hear God's voice in the cries of the poor and alienated. Faith opens our hearts to know that God's treasure of love and goodness abides in the heart of everyone.

Ponder: What do I treasure?

Prayer: Lord, you are always here with me. Deliver me from my fears and grant me the faith to fulfill your law of love.

Ponder: Today I'll be faithful by surrendering to God and letting go of all worries.

Saturday of the Eleventh Week in Ordinary Time

YEAR I
2 Corinthians 12:1–10
Psalm 34:8–9, 10–11, 12–13

YEAR II
2 Chronicles 24:17–25
Psalm 89:4–5, 29–30, 31–32, 33–34

YEARS I AND II
Matthew 6:24–34

[Jesus taught them, saying,] "Look at the birds of the air; they neither sow nor reap nor gather into barns, and yet your heavenly Father feeds them. Are you not of more value than they?"

MATTHEW 6:26

Reflection: We think we must do more, achieve more, produce more to prove our value. We think we must give back by volunteering, participating in fundraisers, or taking part in walks to support worthy causes. We think our lives will be judged useful or not useful according to the list of accomplishments in our resumé.

Yet Jesus tells us we're of more value than the birds that live freely—soaring high, adapting to the rhythms of the seasons, and being fed by God's abundance in nature. We have been given the gift of life, made in God's image of love and goodness, and are beloved of God just because we are. God freely pours out love and blessings on us. We do not have to earn God's love. We do not have to give back to God. We do not have to worry about who we are.

Sometimes people we know give us the message that we aren't enough. Sometimes people will tell us they love us and then put conditions on that love. It isn't that way with God. God loves us just the way we are, even when we mistakenly think we're not enough. Every day God gives us everything we need for that day so that we may be messengers of God's hope and peace.

We can stop worrying. We can have faith in our intrinsic goodness and worth as precious children of God and pass on to others what we have received: God's love, compassion, and forgiveness.

Ponder: What do I worry about?

Prayer: Lord, you bless me with abundant gifts. Grant me the faith to know you will give me everything I need today.

Practice: Today I will be faithful by watching the birds of the air.

Twelfth Sunday
in Ordinary Time

YEAR A

Jeremiah 20:10–13
Psalm 69:8–10, 14, 17, 33–35
Romans 5:12–15
Matthew 10:26–33

"Are not two sparrows sold for a penny? Yet not one of them will fall to the ground apart from your Father. And even the hairs of your head are all counted. So do not be afraid; you are of more value than many sparrows."

MATTHEW 10:29–31

Reflection: We can become too self-consumed and too preoccupied with our own little world. We take good care ourselves and our material possessions. We maintain our homes and cars on a regular basis. We update our wardrobes. We keep careful watch over our financial accounts. We stress over our image and worry about what others think. Our chronic selfishness blinds us to the needs and concerns of others. Our hearts are absent of care and compassion.

Throughout the world, people fall to the ground and die from lack of basic care. Our unconcern for others makes it easier for the demon of indifference to overtake the world. Life is endangered when we stop caring for one another: The earth is destroyed, people fight against each other, families fall apart, children are neglected, the elderly are abandoned, the poor are despised, strangers are turned away, the uninsured die, the illiterate are lost, and the undocumented are deported.

In God's eyes, every person is created with equal value; every person deserves respect and care. We must see and care for all people as God sees and cares for them. We've been placed on this earth to love and care for each other. We're connected to people from all walks of life. We possess a common life given to us by God. We have a common responsibility to care for this life and to help each other live a good and fruitful life.

Ponder: What is the source of my selfishness?

Prayer: Lord, your gift of unselfish love redeems the world. Remove the selfishness from my heart so I can love and care for others.

Practice: Today I will be faithful by showing care to a person in need.

YEAR B

Job 38:1, 8–11
Psalm 107:23–24, 25–26, 28–29, 30–31
2 Corinthians 5:14–17
Mark 4:35–41

"Teacher, do you not care that we are perishing?" He woke up and rebuked the wind, and said to the sea, "Peace! Be still!" Then the wind ceased, and there was a dead calm. He said to them, "Why are you afraid? Have you still no faith?"

MARK 4:38B–40

Reflection: The storms of life come upon us in different ways. The sudden death of a loved one turns our world upside down; we are tossed about by the emotional winds of grief and loss. Living in an abusive situation is an unpredictable, stressful, terrifying experience. Betrayal creates a whirlwind of inner turmoil and self-doubt; it destroys our confidence and ability to trust. Job loss has catastrophic consequences for families who consequently lose health insurance, their home, and their children's college funds.

We are also confronted by cosmic storms that bring about more destruction and death. The HIV/AIDS pandemic consumes thousands of lives. Poverty, famine, and disease have not yet been rebuked by food, clean water, and medicines. Misguided leaders support violence and war as the way to peace and security.

We're always in the midst of some type of storm, but people of faith know that God is always with them and that God's power quiets the violent, destructive, and terrifying forces of life. Faith means that our relationship with God can't be destroyed by external forces. People of faith can withstand the storms of life and winds of change. We have the power of God in us to work together to quiet the storms of global poverty and to still world violence.

Ponder: What is the nature of my storm?

Prayer: Lord, you bring compassion and peace to a fragile world. Strengthen my faith and help me trust your presence.

Practice: Today I will be faithful by being calm and trusting when life becomes chaotic.

YEAR C

Zechariah 12:10–11; 13:1
Psalm 63:2, 3–4, 5–6, 8–9
Galatians 3:26–29
Luke 9:18–24

"If any want to become my followers, let them deny themselves and take up their cross daily and follow me."

LUKE 9:23B

Reflection: Following a diet requires us to commit to a specific plan and be disciplined enough to follow it. People on a diet have to deny themselves certain foods. People in recovery from substance abuse must be committed to a program and follow the Twelve Steps; they must say no daily to people, places, and things that might cause them to relapse.

Following Christ isn't like a diet plan or recovery program. Following Christ is a trust-walk shaped and informed by Jesus' life and teachings. Following Christ requires us to say no to worldly possessions, personal success, and power and to say yes to a simple lifestyle, self-renunciation, and humble service. Following Christ ultimately means living as Christ lived, sharing the love, compassion, forgiveness, and peace of God with all people. Following Christ challenges us to sometimes say no to watching television, playing computer games, and shopping to make time for solitude, Scripture, and prayer.

Learning to say no requires discernment and the discipline of a daily practice. When we say no to self-destructive behavior, we become healthy and feel better about ourselves. When we say no to negative attitudes, we have a more positive outlook. When we say no to material things, we can be attentive to spiritual matters. When we say no to instant self-gratification, we're free to love and care for others, especially the poor.

Ponder: What do I need to say no to?

Prayer: Lord, you gave your life as a gift of love for the whole world. Help me be a selfless servant of your love, compassion, and peace.

Practice: Today I will be faithful by volunteering to work at a soup kitchen.

Monday of the Twelfth Week in Ordinary Time

YEAR I
Genesis 12:1–9
Psalm 33:12–13, 18–19, 20 and 22

YEAR II
2 Kings 17:5–8, 13–15, 18
Psalm 60:3, 4–5, 12–13

YEARS I AND II
Matthew 7:1–5

[Jesus taught them, saying,] "Do not judge, so that you may not be judged."

MATTHEW 7:1

Reflection: Jesus calls us to let go of judgment, blame, and finger-pointing. He calls us to face our human weaknesses with compassion and a willingness to be transformed. He calls us to be aware of our own attitudes, behaviors, and thoughts and to ask God to heal us of everything that prevents us from loving ourselves and our neighbors.

Any time we're tempted to judge others, we must remember that we, too, wrestle with human emotions, desires, and needs and that sometimes we don't make the most loving choices. As we seek to be more like Jesus in our acceptance of ourselves and others, we must be aware of the negative ways we speak to ourselves and others. Choosing nonjudgmental words when we express ourselves means avoiding words such as "should," "lazy," and "useless."

Letting go of negative judgment gives us the freedom to dialogue with God, ourselves, and others without fear and without shame. Judging shuts down our ability to connect at an intimate level. Letting go of judgment opens us to endless possibilities of exploration, creativity, and knowledge. Judging prevents us from admitting our inner fears. Letting go of judgment allows us to be curious, to wonder, and to experience the fullness of life and love.

As we refrain from judgment, we become more accepting of ourselves and others. We have a growing awareness of the goodness and love in our hearts and we learn to see, recognize, and rejoice in that same goodness and love in others.

Ponder: When have I judged others?

Prayer: Lord, you see me with eyes of compassionate acceptance. Help me let go of my need to judge myself and others.

Practice: Today I will be faithful by not using the word *should*.

Tuesday of the Twelfth Week
in Ordinary Time

YEAR I
Genesis 13:2, 5–18
Psalm 15:2–3a, 3bc–4ab, 5

YEAR II
2 Kings 19:9b–11, 14–21, 31–35a, 36
Psalm 48:2–3, 3–4,10–11

YEARS I AND II
Matthew 7:6, 12–14

[Jesus taught them, saying,] "In everything do to others as you would have them do to you; for this is the law and the prophets."

MATTHEW 7:12

Reflection: We know the right thing to do. We know that choosing love over hate is the right thing to do. We know that choosing peace over war is the right thing to do. We know that choosing forgiveness over resentment is the right thing to do.

Yet even when we know we have a choice, sometimes we find it hard to make the choice that reflects the law of love. We're conflicted by our desire for security, comfort, and autonomy. We find it hard to loosen our hold on material possessions, intellectual property, and financial stability. We're afraid to change our lifestyles, our habits, and our traditions.

Jesus teaches us to make our choices by putting ourselves in others' shoes. If we're visiting an elderly relative: What if *we* were old and forgetful? How would *we* want to be treated?

If we're speaking to someone who doesn't understand English: What if *we* were in a country where we didn't speak the language? How would *we* want to be treated?

If we're thinking of firing an employee: What if *we* were about to lose our job? How would *we* want to be treated?

If we're asked to vote for laws that open the way to kill those whose physical or mental conditions are expensive to manage: What if *we* were ill? How would *we* want to be treated?

How do *we* want to be treated? With respect. With kindness. With understanding. With courtesy. With generosity. With acceptance. With compassion. With love.

Ponder: How do I treat others?

Prayer: Lord, you are compassion and love. Help me choose love and compassion when relating to my sisters and brothers.

Practice: Today I will be faithful by doing to others as I would have them do to me.

Wednesday of the Twelfth Week in Ordinary Time

YEAR I
Genesis 15:1–12, 17–18
Psalm 105:1–2, 3–4, 6–7, 8–9

YEAR II
2 Kings 22:8–13, 23:1–3
Psalm 119:33, 34, 35, 36, 37, 40

YEARS I AND II
Matthew 7:15–20

"A good tree cannot bear bad fruit, nor can a bad tree bear good fruit."

MATTHEW 7:18

Reflection: We are good. Human nature is endowed with goodness. We have a duty to be good, but we must intend to be good and show goodness. We have the potential to love, but we have to intend to love and share love with others. We have the capacity to care, but we have to intend to care and show care to others. People know who we are and what is in our hearts by the fruit we bear.

It is unreasonable for good people to be abusive and violent toward another human being. It goes against human nature to hate people, to destroy life, to disrespect the environment, to ignore people in need, to incite violence and war, and to deny people freedom. A voice inside us constantly calls us to be true to our human nature—to be good.

Our basic struggle is being consistently good toward all people. People of faith have been taught a fundamental truth—*every person is created in the image and likeness of God.* This translates into an understanding that God is the source and foundation of all that is good. We are godlike when we choose and demonstrate goodness. People of faith can draw on the wisdom of Jesus found in the gospels to live a good life. We can share this wisdom with believers and nonbelievers because being good is at the heart of what it means to be an authentic person.

Ponder: How do I share my goodness with others?

Prayer: Lord, you revealed the goodness of God through your words and deeds. Open my eyes to see your divine goodness in myself and in the hearts of all people.

Practice: Today I will be faithful by affirming something good in the people I meet.

Thursday of the Twelfth Week in Ordinary Time

YEAR I
Genesis 16:1–12, 15–16
Psalm 106:1b–2, 3–4a, 4b–5

YEAR II
2 Kings 24:8–17
Psalm 79:1b–2, 3–5, 8, 9

YEARS I AND II
Matthew 7:21–29

[Jesus taught them, saying,] "Not everyone who says to me, 'Lord, Lord,' will enter the kingdom of heaven, but only the one who does the will of my Father in heaven."

MATTHEW 7:21

Reflection: We needn't wait to experience the kingdom of heaven. The kingdom of heaven exists wherever and whenever we're doing God's will.

We make the kingdom of heaven apparent when we humbly ask God to show us what to do in the moment. Any time we feel perplexed, stuck, depressed, or uncertain, we just need to ask God what to do next. With faith that God answers us, we can move on, trusting we're in the space of God's will.

We make the kingdom of God apparent when we do our best to follow Jesus' example of love, peace, and forgiveness. Our willingness to be the love-bearer, the peacemaker, and the reconciler has a tremendous impact for good in our world.

We make the kingdom of God apparent when we set aside our own needs of the moment and pay attention to someone who is troubled, lonely, or discouraged. Our ability to bring a compassionate heart, a listening ear, and an encouraging presence to those in need brings light to the darkness.

Doing God's will is as simple as finding ways to love ourselves and our neighbors. Whenever we feel too tired, too stubborn, or too arrogant to choose the way of love, we know we need to come back to our God-center and humbly ask to be shown the next right thing to do.

Ponder: What is God's will for me today?

Prayer: Lord, you are always at my side. Bless me with the knowledge of your will for me. Help me carry it out.

Practice: Today I will be faithful by asking God to show me what to do and how to do it.

Friday of the Twelfth Week in Ordinary Time

YEAR I

Genesis 17:1, 9–10, 15–22
Psalm 128:1–2, 3, 4–5

YEAR II

2 Kings 25:1–12
Psalm 137:1–2, 3, 4–5, 6

YEARS I AND II

Matthew 8:1–4

And there was a leper who came to [Jesus] and knelt before him, saying, "Lord, if you choose, you can make me clean." He stretched out his hand and touched him, saying, "I do choose. Be made clean!" Immediately his leprosy was cleansed.

MATTHEW 8:2B–3

Reflection: We need the faith of the leper, an outcast in his society who dares to approach Jesus and ask for healing. Whatever our failings, whatever secrets we harbor that make us feel unclean, whatever illness or infirmity we suffer, we can approach Jesus in faith and ask to be made whole again. Jesus will never refuse our request. Jesus always meets us where we are.

We need Jesus' compassion to respond to those who ask for our help. However burdened, depleted, or overwhelmed we feel, we must draw on the spirit of empathy that leads us to identify with those in need of comfort and encouragement. Our willingness to set aside our own cares to help someone demonstrates our desire to be more like Jesus.

We need Jesus' generosity to stretch out loving and encouraging hands and touch the lives and hearts of those we encounter. We need to learn to look beyond the face presented to us. However repellent someone may seem, underneath the skin color, illness, decrepitude, neediness, aggression, or narcissism is a precious child of God in need of love and compassion.

We're all God's children. We all need a healing touch. We're all capable of bringing the touch of respect, kindness, and comfort to each other.

Ponder: When have I felt unclean?

Prayer: Lord, your touch is gentle and loving. Heal me of all that prevents me from seeing my sisters and brothers with eyes of love.

Practice: Today I will be faithful by encouraging all those who approach me.

Saturday of the Twelfth Week in Ordinary Time

YEAR I

Genesis 18:1–15
Psalm LUKE *1:46–47, 48–49, 50, 53, 54–55*

YEAR II

Lamentations 2:2, 10–14, 18–19
Psalm 74:1b–2, 3–5, 5–7, 20–21

YEARS I AND II

Matthew 8:5–17

And to the centurion Jesus said, "Go; let it be done for you according to your faith." And the servant was healed in that hour.

MATTHEW 8:13

Reflection: With what degree of faith do we approach the Lord? How certain are we that God is listening to us? What is our level of trust in God's care and love?

Often it seems that our prayers are designed to direct God: *Please heal my sister-in-law. Please sober up my nephew. Please send money to pay the bills. Please make this pain go away. Please bring my brother back to church. Please find me a job.*

There is no need to direct God. Like the centurion, we can just present our situation to God. And God will help us. Our challenge is to let go of the outcome and have faith that God will indeed respond in the best possible way for us.

Sometimes our biggest act of faith is in not knowing what to ask for. We approach God humbly, seeking only knowledge of God's will for us and the grace to carry it out. We present our lives to God with all our worries, insecurities, anxieties, and responsibilities. We acknowledge our limitations and our strengths and confess our dependence on God. We may not know what to ask for, but we do know we need God's guidance and love.

This "not knowing" opens into endless possibilities. Our willingness to let God act in our best interest brings new insights, spiritual adventures, interesting events, and deep fulfillment. We become more aware of God's presence, feeling God's nearness in every breath. We grow in faith. We trust that all is well.

Ponder: How has my faith grown?

Prayer: Lord, you are always near. Deepen my faith in your goodness and love so I may be a sign of faith.

Practice: Today I will be faithful by praying without telling God what to do.

Thirteenth Sunday
in Ordinary Time

YEAR A

2 Kings 4:8–11, 14–16a
Psalm 89:2–3, 16–17, 18–19
Romans 6:3–4, 8–11
Matthew 10:37–42

"Whoever loves father or mother more than me is not worthy of me; and whoever loves son or daughter more than me is not worthy of me; and whoever does not take up the cross and follow me is not worthy of me."

MATTHEW 10:37–38

Reflection: It's difficult to let go of the things we cherish. We usually want more of what we already possess: more food, more money, more clothes, another house, another car, more perks. We work hard to look prosperous and successful. We enjoy living comfortably and wouldn't have it any other way.

It's even more difficult to let go of the people we love. We have strong ties to our families and friends. We work hard to love the members of our family, to earn their trust, and to maintain good relationships with them. We enjoy the friendships we've made and can't imagine being without them. Some of the greatest moments are the ones we spend with family and friends.

As people of faith, we're asked to value our relationship with Jesus more than family, friends, and possessions. We're asked to surrender all we have, take up the cross, and follow Jesus. We live in a culture that thrives on the belief that the good life is something we find for ourselves rather than something we lose for the sake of Jesus.

Following Jesus demands some lifestyle changes. We must create more space and time for solitude and prayer. We must buy fewer things so we can give more to the poor. We must remind family members and friends that our relationship with Jesus is worth dying for.

Ponder: What am I afraid to lose?

Prayer: Lord, your death on the cross brought life to the world. Help me follow your example of selfless love.

Practice: Today I will be faithful by spending quiet time with Jesus in prayer.

YEAR B

Wisdom 1:13–15; 2:23–24
Psalm 30:2, 4, 5–6, 11, 12, 13
2 Corinthians 8:7, 9, 13–15
Mark 5:21–43

God did not make death, and he does not delight in the death of the living. For he created all things so that they might exist.

WISDOM 1:13–14

Reflection: We don't delight in keeping vigil with a dying loved one. We don't delight in the sudden death of friends and colleagues who have committed suicide. We don't delight in seeing children throughout the world waste away because of a lack of food and clean water. We don't delight in knowing that thousands of people who live with HIV/AIDS will die because there are no hospitals and clinics to care for them. We don't delight in teenagers' destroying their lives with drugs. We don't delight in the suffering of victims of human trafficking, genocide, conflicts, violence, and war. We don't delight in a friend's painful divorce or a neighbor's loss of job or home. We don't delight in any situation that harms people or robs them of life.

We believe human life is a precious gift from God. This fundamental truth must never be denied. Every person is given life and, with it, the responsibility to defend and protect life from all forms of destruction.

We will be tested by mental, emotional, spiritual, and physical pain. The suffering we experience on our journey becomes an opportunity to invite others to reflect with us on the deeper meaning of life.

Life is a mystery that unfolds one moment at a time. We are called to embrace the mystery and delight in living one day at a time.

Ponder: What do I enjoy about my life?

Prayer: Lord, you promise eternal life to all who believe in you. Give me the courage to be an advocate for life.

Practice: Today I will be faithful by encouraging others not to take life for granted.

YEAR C

1 Kings 19:16b, 19–21
Psalm 16:1–2, 5, 7–8, 9–10, 11
Galatians 5:1, 13–18
Luke 9:51–62

For you were called to freedom, brothers and sisters; only do not use your freedom as an opportunity for self-indulgence, but through love become slaves to one another. For the whole law is summed up in a single commandment, "You shall love your neighbor as yourself."

Galatians 5:13–14

Reflection: Freedom is an essential characteristic of what it means to be a person. We cherish our individual freedom, our right to free speech and free assembly. Freedom empowers us to work for the common good of all people. Whenever external forces attempt to control, limit, or deny us freedom, we rally to voice our opposition.

We cannot have freedom without personal responsibility. We are not free to do what we please at the expense of others. We are not free to destroy human life, to squander the earth's resources, to disregard others' dignity and freedom, to ignore the needs of the poor, and to inflict harm. Freedom without personal responsibility disrupts social progress and threatens human existence.

People of faith see freedom as a gift and calling from God. With God's freedom, we are liberated from selfishness and empowered to love and serve others. We are liberated from the limitations of the material world. We have access to the transforming grace of the kingdom of God to free people from oppressive, imprisoning situations. We come to understand true freedom as the ability to accept unreservedly the unconditional love of God and the responsibility to share this love with all people. When we embrace God's freedom, we fulfill God's command: "You shall love your neighbor as yourself."

Ponder: How do I use my freedom?

Prayer: Lord, by your cross and resurrection you set us free. Liberate me from the prison of selfishness and empower me to lovingly serve my brothers and sisters.

Practice: Today I will be faithful by using my freedom to be a positive influence on others.

Monday of the Thirteenth Week in Ordinary Time

YEAR I

Genesis 18:16–33
Psalm 103:1b–2, 3–4, 8–9, 10–11

YEAR II

Amos 2:6–10, 13–16
Psalm 50:16bc–17, 18–19, 20–21, 22–23

YEARS I AND II

Matthew 8:18–22

Another of [Jesus'] disciples said to him,
"Lord, first let me go and bury my father."
But Jesus said to him, "Follow me, and let
the dead bury their own dead."

MATTHEW 8:21–22

Reflection: Our rituals around death are designed to help those who must now face life without a loved one's tangible presence. Our rituals show our respect for the physical remains of the one who has died, giving dignity to the temple that once housed the spirit of one of God's beloved children. Our rituals gather us to offer our memories of the one who has died, to reach out to comfort the bereaved, and to show our compassion and support in a time of sorrow and grief.

Our humanness often limits our ability to let go in faith of those who have died. We mourn because we can no longer see our loved ones, hear their voices, touch their hands. We mourn because our lives feel empty, we're afraid of change, and we don't feel safe. In effect, we mourn for ourselves, not for our loved ones.

With faith in Jesus and his resurrection, we have no need to worry about the dead. The dead are in God's compassionate care. The dead are on a mysterious journey we can only guess at, hope for, and believe in.

Our challenge is to let go of our beloved dead. Our challenge is to live each day in faith that we, too, are called and cared for in every moment. Our challenge is to have the faith to live fully and to follow Jesus on the path of compassion and unconditional love.

Ponder: How do I mourn my losses?

Prayer: Lord, you are kind and merciful. Help me live without fear of death and dying.

Practice: Today I will be faithful by sitting in peace with someone who is ill.

Tuesday of the Thirteenth Week in Ordinary Time

YEAR I
Genesis 19:15–29
Psalm 26:2–3, 9–10, 11–12

YEAR II
Amos 3:1–8; 4:11–12
Psalm 5:4b–6a, 6b–7, 8

YEARS I AND II
Matthew 8:23–27

"What sort of man is this, that even the winds and the sea obey him?"

MATTHEW 8:27

Reflection: Each of us is concerned with being a certain kind of person. We are preoccupied with self-image and the way others perceive us. We are careful about how we speak and act in our relationships; we want to be known as principled, fair-minded, sincere, trustworthy, and respectable. We want people to sense in us a pure and loving heart.

We cause confusion in our relationships when our words and actions are incompatible. To say we're people of love but then show hatred to people from different racial backgrounds is hypocritical. To say we're concerned for the poor but then refuse to contribute to a charity is dishonest. To say we're consistently pro-life but then support physician-assisted suicide and the death penalty is contradictory. To say we're peaceful but then never speak out against violence is superficial.

People of faith must be concerned about being in the image of God and imitating the life of Jesus portrayed in the gospels. Believers and unbelievers alike have difficulty embracing the spiritual life when we ignore the teachings on love and forgiveness, fail to show compassionate service to those in need, or don't believe in our hearts the Word of God. We're called to speak and act in ways that reflect intimacy with God and knowledge of God's teachings. We can't expect others to listen to us and follow us if our lives don't correspond to the Word of God.

Ponder: What sort of person do I want to be?

Prayer: Lord, you are the Word of God sent to transform the world. Purify my heart so my words and actions reflect your will.

Practice: Today I will be faithful by letting my actions and words reflect love, compassion, and understanding.

Wednesday of the Thirteenth Week in Ordinary Time

YEAR I
Genesis 21:5, 8–20a
Psalm 34:7–8, 10–11, 12–13

YEAR II
Amos 5:14–15, 21–24
Psalm 50:7, 8–9, 10–11, 12–13, 16bc–17

YEARS I AND II
Matthew 8:28–34

When [Jesus] came to the other side, to the country of the Gadarenes, two demoniacs coming out of the tombs met him.

MATTHEW 8:28

Reflection: We have nothing to fear from coming to meet a kind and loving God. We can feel free to bring all of our demons—our errors, our misdeeds, our failures, our defects of character—to God and know that God will treat us tenderly and kindly. God never abandons us. God loves us just as we are, with all our imperfections, talents, and gifts.

All that we are is a gift from God. Yet all too often we're ashamed of our imperfections. We see our mistakes and feel we're flawed beyond repair. Sometimes we're possessed by negative thinking. When we become aware of our mental, emotional, physical, or spiritual limitations, we trust that God's Spirit is moving to transform us and help us embrace a new way of being.

All that we are is a gift from God. We need to feel free to bring our talents and strengths to God too. Each of us has unique gifts to share. We can spend time in prayer and meditation to discern how best to use them. We have all we need to make a positive difference.

Our challenge always is to listen to the Spirit and go where it leads us. It may feel like we're diving off a cliff into the unknown, but with faith in God's goodness and love, we find the courage to take the plunge.

Ponder: What am I afraid to bring to God?

Prayer: Lord, you have made me in your image of goodness and love. I offer you all my weakness and all my strength. Show me how to use them to help others.

Practice: Today I will be faithful by presenting myself to God in prayer.

Thursday of the Thirteenth Week in Ordinary Time

YEAR I
Genesis 22:1b–19
Psalm 115:1–2, 3–4, 5–6, 8–9

YEAR II
Amos 7:10–17
Psalm 19:8, 9, 10, 11

YEARS I AND II
Matthew 9:1–8

And just then some people were carrying a paralyzed man lying on a bed. When Jesus saw their faith, he said to the paralytic, "Take heart, son; your sins are forgiven."

MATTHEW 9:2

Reflection: Sickness is a universal experience; it is part of the human condition. When we're sick, we're reminded that life is fragile and we need to take good care of ourselves. The experience of illness slows us down, limits our capacity to thrive, and forces us to reassess our priorities. The experience of illness also makes us aware of our dependency on others for love, support, and encouragement. We draw strength from the people who care for us and tend to our needs.

When sickness leaves us, we feel liberated or forgiven from a great burden; we have renewed strength to move forward. As we resume our daily routine, we forget that many people are still burdened with sickness caused by malnutrition, contaminated water, pollution, disease, AIDS, cancer, and mental illness. Many people long to be liberated from the burden of sickness so they can be productive.

People of faith live through the lens of the resurrection. We believe the resurrection gives hope to all people and makes all things new. We're called to share the message of the resurrection with the sick and the poor. As an act of unconditional love, we are to bring the needs of the sick and poor to God through prayer and do whatever we can to comfort them.

Ponder: How do I deal with sickness?

Prayer: Lord, your love heals the brokenness in the world. Help me be a healing presence of love and compassion to all people.

Practice: Today I will be faithful by visiting someone who isn't feeling well.

Friday of the Thirteenth Week in Ordinary Time

YEAR I
Genesis 23:1–4, 19; 24:1–8, 62–67
Psalm 106:1b–2, 3–4a, 4b–5

YEAR II
Amos 8:4–6, 9–12
Psalm 119:2, 10, 20, 30, 40, 131

YEARS I AND II
Matthew 9:9–13

[Jesus said], "Go and learn what this means, 'I desire mercy, not sacrifice.'"

MATTHEW 9:13

Reflection: Mercy is a quality we're called to cultivate as followers of Jesus. Mercy is kin to compassion; it's an understanding of the human condition, of human suffering. Out of our understanding comes our willingness to forgive, reconcile, and be at peace with one another.

Each of us suffers in different ways. We experience physical pain. We experience the sorrow of death. We experience the disappointment of not being chosen for a promotion or a special role. We experience self-doubt when others tell us we're not trustworthy. We experience loneliness when others reject us. We experience resentment when others treat us disrespectfully. We experience anger when others ignore our needs.

Every instance of suffering gives us the opportunity to learn more about who we are in relationship to God. We can focus on remembering that we are beloved of God, made in God's image of goodness and love. We can choose to trust that we are where God needs us to be. We can name our suffering, face it courageously, and not hide behind denial or blame. We can actively seek the positive in what we're experiencing. We can learn to recognize others' suffering and realize we're not alone.

We're called to heed the gospel message and imbed it deeply into our way of being. It is God's will that we love one another and treat all people with mercy, compassion, and love. Jesus doesn't call us to sacrifice anything but our self-will.

Ponder: How do I show mercy?

Prayer: Lord, your mercy endures forever. Help me be merciful in my relations with others.

Practice: Today I will be faithful by forgiving someone who has hurt me.

Saturday of the Thirteenth Week in Ordinary Time

YEAR I

Genesis 27:1–5, 15–29
Psalm 135:1b–2, 3–4, 5–6

YEAR II

Amos 9:11–15
Psalm 85:9ab and 10, 11–12, 13–14

YEARS I AND II

Matthew 9:14–17

Then the disciples of John came to him, saying, "Why do we and the Pharisees fast often, but your disciples do not fast?"

MATTHEW 9:14

Reflection: John's disciples are comparing their practice of fasting to Jesus' disciples' practice of nonfasting. Jesus refuses the comparison, making it clear that his way is not John's or the Pharisees' way.

Comparisons generally result in someone's feeling aggrieved, ashamed, or unworthy. We compare lifestyles and feel envious or entitled. We compare volunteer efforts and feel inadequate or smug. We compare mental abilities and feel inferior or superior. We compare faith and feel insufficient or self-satisfied. We compare cultures and feel embarrassed or arrogant. We compare careers and feel deficient or condescending.

The only comparison we can legitimately make is to ourself. Do we take better care of ourselves than we used to? Are we kinder? Are we less selfish? Do we show more respect to our family members? Are we more patient with the elderly? Are we less apt to offer negative criticism? Are we more generous with our time and resources? Are we slower to offer unsolicited advice? Do we gossip less? Are we spending more time with God? Are we reading holy Scripture more often? Are we learning to love more and fear less?

We are each other's teachers, and we are each other's students. We have much to learn from each other, yet no one knows more than anyone else. We've all been made in God's image of love and goodness. We've all been given everything we need to witness to God's love. We've all been given unique gifts and talents to use to build God's kingdom of love, compassion, and peace.

Ponder: When do I compare myself to others?

Prayer: Lord, you trust me to do your work of love. Help me trust myself.

Practice: Today I will be faithful by avoiding comparisons.

Fourteenth Sunday in Ordinary Time

YEAR A

Zechariah 9:9–10
Psalm 145:1–2, 8–9, 10–11, 13–14
Romans 8:9, 11–13
Matthew 11:25–30

"Come to me, all you that are weary and are carrying heavy burdens, and I will give you rest. Take my yoke upon you, and learn from me; for I am gentle and humble in heart, and you will find rest for your souls. For my yoke is easy, and my burden is light."

MATTHEW 11:28–30

Reflection: We find no peace in situations that cause overwhelming stress. We feel abused in the workplace when coworkers expect us to carry the entire load. We get frustrated with colleagues and friends who burden us with their problems. We become paralyzed from carrying around personal baggage and secrets. We panic when we don't have the resources to meet our financial obligations. When life's burdens become too difficult to bear, we risk having a mental, emotional, spiritual, and physical breakdown.

Society adds to our stress and anxiety every day with a steady flow of messages promoting unhealthy behavior. We're conditioned to keep busy, to stay connected to our friends on the Internet, to seek comfort at the mall, to go out to fast-food restaurants, to spend hours driving from one event to the next, and to find satisfaction outside the home. We suffer from chronic burnout because we don't know how to rest.

People of faith honor the Sabbath and keep the Lord's day holy. We need sacred space and time to be with God. We are yoked to the Trinity, the Scriptures, and the teachings of the gospel. We need time to rest with God, to reflect on God's Word, to pray, to renew the mind, heart, soul, and body. We need Sabbath time each week to remind us that we're made in God's image and likeness, that we are very good.

Ponder: What burdens do I carry?

Prayer: Lord, you give rest to the weary of heart. Help me create space in my life to rest in your presence.

Practice: Today I will be faithful by making time to be alone with God.

YEAR B

Ezekiel 2:2–5
Psalm 123:1–2, 2, 3–4
2 Corinthians 12:7–10
Mark 6:1–6

Then Jesus said to them, "Prophets are not without honor, except in their home town, and among their own kin, and in their own house." And he could do no deed of power there, except that he laid his hands on a few sick people and cured them. And he was amazed at their unbelief.

MARK 6:4–6A

Reflection: Rejection is painful; it denies our dignity and innate goodness. We can't bear the thought of being rejected by our family, neighbors, and friends. We feel not good enough, misjudged, abused, and betrayed. When people close to us reject us, we lose self-confidence, become disempowered and depressed. We struggle to move on, fearful of others who might be out to destroy us.

We live and work with people from all walks of life. We're constantly under scrutiny. We're judged on our race, culture, ethnic background, gender, language, religious tradition, and way of life. We're unjustly criticized by others because we don't support their beliefs, opinions, and ideas. We're ostracized because we don't have the right look.

We look suspicious to others who don't know our personal history and are intimidated by our gifts and talents. We can't progress in a climate of hostility and opposition.

People of faith face the possibility of rejection in giving witness to the gospel. Some people reject God's presence; they refuse to listen to the gospel and deny the power of nonviolence, compassion, and love to transform the world. In the midst of unbelief, confusion, despair, and opposing forces, we're called to be faithful to the gospel and to give witness to the truth: God is love.

Ponder: How do I deal with rejection?

Prayer: Lord, you accept everyone with unconditional love. Help me overcome my fear of others so I can love and accept them as you do.

Practice: Today I will be faithful by being nonjudgmental.

YEAR C

Isaiah 66:10–14c
Psalm 66:1–3, 4–5, 6–7, 16, 20
Galatians 6:14–18
Luke 10:1–12, 17–20

"Go on your way. See, I am sending you out like lambs into the midst of wolves. Carry no purse, no bag, no sandals; and greet no one on the road. Whatever house you enter, first say, 'Peace to this house!'"

LUKE 10:3–5

Reflection: We don't usually go into places and situations where we're not invited. We don't associate with strangers out of fear that they might harm us. We avoid dangerous areas where violence is known to occur. We're told not to walk or run alone at night. We're very cautious about our wallets, purses, and other valuable items. World conflicts, abductions, and community violence remind us that we're not always safe and secure.

We admire men and women who wake up each day to potential danger. We respect police officers who respond to domestic violence, the firefighters who respond to raging fires, the paramedics called out in terrible storms to respond to accidents, doctors and nurses called to respond to an outbreak of a fatal disease, the lifeguards called into deep waters to respond to someone drowning, and the volunteers who respond to refugees driven out of their homelands by famine, drought, war, and violence. People from all walks of life respond to situations that endanger their lives as well as the lives of the people they're trying to save.

People of faith are called to live with the predisposition of God's unconditional love, compassion, forgiveness, and peace in a dangerous world. There will always be an element of risk and a situation awaiting a response of love, peace, and compassion.

Ponder: How do I respond to dangerous situations?

Prayer: Lord, your love protects us in times of trouble. Strengthen my faith that I may be a source of strength to others.

Practice: Today I will be faithful by supporting someone in crisis.

Monday of the Fourteenth Week in Ordinary Time

YEAR I

Genesis 28:10–22a
Psalm 91:1–2, 3–4, 14–15ab

YEAR II

Hosea 2:16, 17c–18, 21–22
Psalm 145:2–3, 4–5, 6–7, 8–9

YEARS I AND II

Matthew 9:18–26

Then suddenly a woman who had been suffering from hemorrhages for twelve years came up behind him and touched the fringe of his cloak, for she said to herself, "If I only touch his cloak, I will be made well."

MATTHEW 9:20–21

Reflection: It takes only a moment, the right moment, when faith opens our heart and we reach out to the Lord for healing in humility and hope. It takes only a moment, the right moment, for the Lord to respond to our need for healing. We sometimes experience instant relief; we sometimes wait for twelve years. Ultimately we receive the healing we were born for, in God's time, at the right moment, when we're ready.

We can rest secure in our faith that God hears our cries for help. We can step into the tranquility of letting go of anxiety about whatever bothers us. We can walk into the unknown that is faith and know that all is well, that all shall be well, and that we're right where we need to be.

A gentle touch of Jesus' robe is all it takes for healing to manifest. The faith behind our touch lives strong and confident in God's love and compassion. The faith behind the touch knows we're beloved, precious, and worthy of God's healing. The faith behind the touch trusts in God's timing, mercy, and all-knowingness. The faith behind the touch allows God to guide us every moment of every day. The faith behind the touch fills our heart with gratitude for God's goodness. The faith behind the touch brings us to our knees in humble thanksgiving for God's attention and compassion.

Ponder: What moves me to reach out to Jesus?

Prayer: Lord, your greatness is unsearchable. Increase my faith that I may await your healing with trust and serenity.

Practice: Today I will be faithful by asking the Lord for healing.

Tuesday of the Fourteenth Week in Ordinary Time

YEAR I

Genesis 32:23–33
Psalm 17:1b, 2–3, 6–7ab, 8b and 15

YEAR II

Hosea 8:4–7, 11–13
Psalm 115:3–4, 5–6, 7ab–8, 9–10

YEARS I AND II

Matthew 9:32–38

Then [Jesus] said to his disciples, "The harvest is plentiful, but the laborers are few; therefore ask the Lord of the harvest to send out laborers into his harvest."

MATTHEW 9:37–38

Reflection: Billions of people live in our world. God loves each of us, calls us by name, knows our needs, knows the longings of our hearts, answers our prayers with compassion, and forgives our transgressions. It's a very big picture: the billions of people milling around the world like lost sheep and the mystery of the one God who loves each of us so extravagantly.

This is the harvest we're invited to join as laborers. We're invited by Jesus to befriend others, to show kindness and compassion, forgiveness and mercy, generosity and helpfulness with our words, thoughts, actions, and way of being. We're called to labor on behalf of God so that each of the world's billions will have faith in God's presence and will feel less lost, less harassed, and less helpless.

To be a laborer in the Lord's harvest is to love our neighbors as we love ourselves. Although we can't hope to touch billions of people, we can be intentional about loving just one person every day.

The mystery of love is that it multiplies the more we share it. The mystery of love is that it impacts the hearts and minds of others in positive, lasting ways we may never know about. The mystery of love is that we give it freely, expect no returns, and yet are continually blessed by love.

Ponder: How do I labor in the Lord's harvest?

Prayer: Lord, you are the good shepherd who leads me on the path of truth and life. Help me sow kindness and love in the hearts of all those I encounter.

Practice: Today I will be faithful by intentionally loving myself and one other person.

Wednesday of the Fourteenth Week in Ordinary Time

YEAR I
Genesis 41:55–57; 42:5–7a, 17–24a
Psalm 33:2–3, 10–11, 18–19

YEAR II
Hosea 10:1–3, 7–8, 12
Psalm 105:2–3, 4–5, 6–7

YEARS I AND II
Matthew 10:1–7

Then Jesus summoned his twelve disciples and gave them authority over unclean spirits, to cast them out, and to cure every disease and every sickness.

MATTHEW 10:1

Reflection: Among the twelve disciples Jesus sends out on a healing mission are fishermen, a tax collector, a doubter, and a betrayer. The Lord makes good use of all people to make manifest the kingdom of God. God's love and healing transcend our small human efforts. God's power works through us to bring compassion, peace, and love to our world. God's wholeness makes us holy as we focus our minds and hearts on living in compassion, living in peace, living in love.

We can never know another person completely, but our faith teaches us that all people everywhere are made in God's image of goodness and love. Whatever characteristics we manifest, whatever personality quirks we display, whatever actions we do, the fundamental truth of our likeness to God never changes.

If we doubt God, if we doubt our goodness, if we doubt others' motives, we're still grounded in God's love. If we betray God, if we betray ourselves, if we betray others, we're still precious children of God. If we lie, cheat, steal, and kill, we've broken our covenant of love with God; yet our true nature, our likeness to God's love and goodness, our status as beloved children of God remains intact.

The mystery of love is that it bears, believes, hopes, and endures all—and never ends. We have been given authority to embody that love for all to know.

Ponder: How do I use my power and authority?

Prayer: Lord, you know all of me and love me just as I am. Bless me with what I need to walk as your disciple in love.

Practice: Today I will be faithful by being a disciple of Jesus' love, compassion, and healing.

Thursday of the Fourteenth Week in Ordinary Time

YEAR I

Genesis 44:18–21, 23–29; 45:1–5
Psalm 105:16–17, 18–19, 20–21

YEAR II

Hosea 11:1–4, 8e–9
Psalm 80:2ac and 3b, 15–16

YEARS I AND II

Matthew 10:7–15

"Cure the sick, raise the dead, cleanse the lepers, cast out demons. You received without payment; give without payment."

MATTHEW 10:8

Reflection: God showers us with love. God loves us unconditionally. God loves us without wanting anything in return. God loves us without expectations. God loves us when we're rude, sarcastic, troublesome, whiny, and manipulative. God loves us when we're kind, respectful, cooperative, cheerful, and collaborative. God is love. God loves—that's what God does.

We receive God's abundant love every moment. Do we practice giving love every moment? Do we give love without conditions or expectations? Do we measure love? Do we love ourselves and others in difficult moments, through difficult moods? Do we save our love for people who do as we wish or who meet our standard of worthiness?

Do we love the modern-day lepers—those living with HIV/AIDS, illegal immigrants, the homeless, the jobless? Do we allow our love to cure the loneliness and fear of the sick?

Do we allow our love to cast out demons of despair, rage, depression, or narcissism? Do we allow our love to cast out demons of conflict, division, or aggression? Do we allow our love to cast out demons of feeling unworthy, ashamed, or of no consequence?

Do we allow our love to raise those whose faith has died, whose self-esteem is crushed, whose hope in humanity is atrophied? Do we allow our love to raise those who are unresponsive to others' needs? Do we allow our love to raise the consciousness of a society that is indifferent to suffering?

God's love is freely given. How freely do we love?

Ponder: Where am I stingy?

Prayer: Lord, you give me everything. Teach me to be generous with your gifts that I may give without expecting payment.

Practice: Today I will be faithful by giving time to a project for the poor.

Friday of the Fourteenth Week in Ordinary Time

YEAR I

Genesis 46:1–7, 28–30
Psalm 37:3–4, 18–19, 27–28, 39–40

YEAR II

Hosea 14:2–10
Psalm 51:3–4, 8–9, 12–13, 14 and 17

YEARS I AND II

Matthew 10:16–23

"See, I am sending you out like sheep into the midst of wolves; so be wise as serpents and innocent as doves."

MATTHEW 10:16

Reflection: Awareness is an important human attribute. We gain wisdom by being aware of our inner world and our environment. We grow in self-understanding when we reflect on the way we process our thoughts, interact with others, and respond to experiences. As we mature, we learn the importance of self-discipline, of setting limits for ourselves to avoid hardship and pain.

Living with awareness helps us discern who we want to be when confronted with personal and social challenges. We often find ourselves pulled into uncomfortable circumstances. When we are confronted by racial hatred, selfishness, greed, oppression, indifference, and violence, we must be self-aware and exercise self-restraint, prudent judgment, and right behavior.

People of faith can't pick and choose the issues and challenges that are worthy of attention. Awareness of the presence of God in all aspects of life is the beginning of spiritual wisdom and the catalyst to be God's instrument of love, compassion, and peace.

Making people aware of the presence of God in difficult moments is not easy. We need courageous hearts to speak God's wisdom in the midst of wolves. We may face many obstacles, hostile responses from others, and rejection for bearing witness to the gospel. With awareness of the risks our faith in God invites, we're not afraid to be what we were called to be: messengers of peace and reconciliation.

Ponder: What wolves am I afraid to confront?

Prayer: Lord, you shepherd us with gentleness and love along safe paths. Help me face challenges with tenderness and kindness.

Practice: Today I will be faithful by being aware of an opportunity to share a message of peace.

Saturday of the Fourteenth Week in Ordinary Time

YEAR I
Genesis 49:29–33; 50:15–26a
Psalm 105:1–2, 3–4, 6–7

YEAR II
Isaiah 6:1–8
Psalm 93:1ab, 1cd–2, 5

YEARS I AND II
Matthew 10:24–33

"What I say to you in the dark, tell in the light; and what you hear whispered, proclaim from the housetops."

MATTHEW 10:27

Reflections: Even when we're too stunned by grief or depression to consciously turn our attention to God for help, God's love and compassion are at work in our hearts. We needn't be afraid of dark moments because God is always there, comforting us and holding us tenderly. In the numbness of our suffering, God whispers love and encouragement, gently leading us to the light of understanding and to the place of acceptance.

As we experience the emergence from dark to light and listen to the comforting God-whispers, our faith in God's compassion deepens. We're aware of

God's personal interest in us. We know God cares about us. We feel more secure and less afraid. We learn to let God take charge. We become less rebellious when difficulties, problems, and sorrows arise.

We trust all is well—in darkness and in the light.

Our deepening faith impacts how we choose to live. Our words and actions reflect the compassion, care, and attention we've received. We become mindful about reaching out to those in need. We dare to visit those who are experiencing dark times—those who are lonely, depressed, ill, addicted, grief-stricken, resentful. We're inspired to speak about our own dark places and our healing. We proclaim the Good News of God's healing that has led us out of the dark of hopelessness into the light of gratitude and compassion.

Ponder: What truth am I afraid to reveal?

Prayer: Lord, you've counted every hair on my head. Give me the faith to proclaim your care and compassion from the housetop of my life.

Practice: Today I will be faithful by reaching out to someone who is experiencing the darkness of loss.

Fifteenth Sunday
in Ordinary Time

YEAR A

Isaiah 55:10–11
Psalm 65:10, 11, 12–13, 14
Romans 8:18–23
Matthew 13:1–23

"So shall my word be that goes out from my mouth; it shall not return to me empty, but it shall accomplish that which I purpose, and succeed in the thing for which I sent it."

ISAIAH 55:11

Reflection: We feel good about ourselves when our intentions and plans have been brought to fruition. Parents are happy when their children reflect what they've learned at home: good manners, self-control, and concern for others. Teachers are proud of their students when they can demonstrate competence in what they've learned. Coaches have confidence in the team when their players execute the plays and drills they've been taught. Parents, teachers, and coaches share a common purpose and goal: to help children and youth maximize their gifts and talents and be successful.

We want people to know and believe they have a purpose. We want them to be able to accomplish what is in their hearts and to succeed in what brings them a sense of personal satisfaction. We need to be more aware of how we influence people's lives. Many people around us think they don't have a purpose; they don't feel good enough to accomplish anything and are afraid to succeed.

People of faith believe God has given the world a universal purpose. As we grow and mature, we discern a vocation, but our calling is to accomplish the will of God: to love one another.

We were created to accomplish the will of God on earth. We can't do God's work alone; we must work together to maximize our gifts and talents to succeed in creating universal love and peace.

Ponder: What is my purpose?

Prayer: Lord, you completed God's work on earth. Help me know and accomplish God's will.

Practice: Today I will be faithful by discerning God's will.

YEAR B

Amos 7:12–15
Psalm 85:9–10, 11–12, 13–14
Ephesians 1:3–14
Mark 6:7–13

[Jesus] called the twelve and began to send them out two by two, and gave them authority over the unclean spirits.

MARK 6:7

Reflection: We respect people with authority. They have power and influence. We recognize traditional roles of authority such as parents, teachers, religious leaders, government leaders, public officials, law-enforcement officers, judges, lawyers, presidents, and executives. We expect people with authority to use their power and influence for the common good, to be responsible, trustworthy, and attentive to the concerns of the people they care for.

People with authority are capable of abusing their power and influence. Without proper oversight, people with authority may feel they're entitled to certain privileges and favors. When people with authority are consumed with power, they can take advantage of people, damaging them mentally, emotionally, spiritually, and physically.

We're aware of the abuse of power on the part of secular and religious leaders throughout the world and its terrible impact on people, communities, and nations. Abuse of power among people with authority has contributed to genocide, sexual exploitation, poverty, sectarian violence, and war.

People of faith believe that all authority comes from God and that this authority is at the service of the gospel. God's authority is always an exercise of love, compassion, forgiveness, and peace. God's authority doesn't overpower people but empowers them to care for the poor, show forgiveness, and work for the common good. At baptism we were given the authority to proclaim the gospel and serve the needs of all.

Ponder: How do I exercise my authority?

Prayer: Lord, you offered your life in humble service to humanity. Empower me with your Spirit, that I may be a humble servant of love and compassion to all people.

Practice: Today I will be faithful by using my authority and power for good.

YEAR C

Deuteronomy 30:10–14
Psalm 69:14, 17, 30–31, 33–34, 36, 37 or
Psalm 19:8, 9, 10, 11
Colossians 1:15–20
Luke 10:25–37

But wanting to justify himself, [a lawyer] asked Jesus, "And who is my neighbor?"

LUKE 10:29

Reflection: A neighbor is someone who lives near us. When we think of neighbors, we think of the people next door, the people we've come to know over time, the familiar people living in our neighborhood. We feel safe in our neighborhood because it's familiar territory. We're comfortable with the people around us.

We enjoy being with people who share our values, principles, beliefs, and interests. We have a special bond with the people who speak our professional language, belong to the same clubs, celebrate our customs and traditions. If our friends have a need, we're ready and willing to help.

The farther we move beyond our street and neighborhood, the more difficult it is to identify our neighbors. We don't think of every person we encounter as a neighbor. We don't see a homeless person as our neighbor. We don't see a poor person as our neighbor. We don't see a person from a different race as our neighbor. We don't see a gay person as our neighbor. We don't see an undocumented person as our neighbor. We don't see an abused person as our neighbor. We don't see anyone outside our immediate neighborhood as our neighbor.

People of faith take the great commandment to heart and are neighbors to all people. We may not have an intimate relationship with everyone in our community, but we do acknowledge everyone as a neighbor. We're called by the gospel not to discriminate but to be near all people who need love, compassion, forgiveness, and understanding.

Ponder: Who is my neighbor?

Prayer: Lord, you are near to the brokenhearted. Help me be a good neighbor to all people.

Practice: Today I will be faithful by being a neighbor to someone I've neglected.

Monday of the Fifteenth Week in Ordinary Time

YEAR I
Exodus 1:8–14, 22
Psalm 124:1b–3, 4–6, 7–8

YEAR II
Isaiah 1:10–17
Psalm 50:8–9, 16bc–17, 21 and 23

YEARS I AND II
Matthew 10:34—11:1

"Whoever welcomes you welcomes me, and whoever welcomes me welcomes the one who sent me."

MATTHEW 10:40

Reflection: Hospitality is a wonderful gift. Some of us have it. We host birthday parties, cookouts, Thanksgiving feasts, and Super Bowl parties. There's always room for one more at our table. We enjoy welcoming others into our home, serving a meal, and exchanging news and ideas. We find great fulfillment in this gift of hospitality.

Others of us are less able to welcome others into our homes. Perhaps we struggle to make ends meet and can't stretch our budget to entertain. Perhaps some family members are unsafe to be around. Perhaps we're afraid no one would enjoy our company.

Whether or not we're able to be hospitable in our homes, we can always offer a gift of welcome to those we encounter. We can welcome others by our smile. We can welcome others by giving up our seat on a crowded bus or train. We can welcome others by holding a door open. We can welcome others by listening to their troubles. We can welcome others by reassuring them that they're beloved children of God and cherished members of our human family. We can welcome others by taking an interest in their lives, celebrating their successes, and supporting them in times of need.

Whenever we extend a welcome to any of our sisters and brothers, we're moving within God's community. We welcome Jesus, our model of love and compassion. We welcome God, the one who sent Jesus to show us the way of humility and truth. And we welcome the Spirit of God, who gives us life and the grace to live it according to God's will.

Ponder: Whom do I refuse to welcome?

Prayer: Lord, you embrace us with tenderness. May I never refuse a welcome to any of my sisters and brothers.

Practice: Today I will be faithful by welcoming everyone I meet.

Tuesday of the Fifteenth Week in Ordinary Time

YEAR I
Exodus 2:1–15a
Psalm 69:3, 14, 30–31, 33–34

YEAR II
Isaiah 7:1–9
Psalm 48:2–3a, 3b–4, 5–6, 7–8

YEARS I AND II
Matthew 11:20–24

Then [Jesus] began to reproach the cities in which most of his deeds of power had been done, because they did not repent.

MATTHEW 11:20

Reflection: Witnessing Jesus' powerful deeds wasn't enough to change the people of Chorazin, Bethsaida, and Capernaum. They still went about business as usual, unrepentant, unwilling to embrace the way of Jesus—the way of love, compassion, and peace.

Living according to God's will that we love one another takes energy and intention. We must make a decision every day—sometimes every moment—to choose kindness, respect, and courtesy. We must stay mindful of our call to compassion, reconciliation, and forgiveness. We must deliberately choose words that encourage, comfort, and promote peace.

We're surrounded by reminders of the power of God in our everyday lives, yet sometimes we still doubt God's goodness, God's love, God's presence. This doubt is something to repent. Doubt blocks us from feeling God's personal care for us. Doubt increases division and conflict. Doubt is at the root of jealousy, envy, and dissatisfaction. Doubt is a threat to healthy relationships and a source of constant stress.

When we keep our attention on living according to God's will, faith begins to replace doubt. Our faith in God's vision of love and unity deepens. Our faith in God's presence in every human person increases. Our faith in ourselves and in our ability to witness to God's love and healing strengthens and transforms our lives.

Ponder: Where do I resist positive change?

Prayer: Lord, you reach out to me in kindness and forgiveness. Heal my doubt in your love. Bless me with the courage to live according to your will.

Practice: Today I will be faithful by recognizing the power of God's healing presence.

Wednesday of the Fifteenth Week in Ordinary Time

YEAR I
Exodus 3:1–6, 9–12
Psalm 103:1b–2, 3–4, 6–7

YEAR II
Isaiah 10:5–7, 13b–16
Psalm 94:5–6, 7–8, 9–10, 14–15

YEARS I AND II
Matthew 11:25–27

Jesus said, "I thank you, Father, Lord of heaven and earth, because you have hidden these things from the wise and the intelligent and have revealed them to infants; yes, Father, for such was your gracious will."

MATTHEW 11:25–26

Reflection: It isn't wisdom or intelligence that will reveal God's will for us. Trust, vulnerability, innocence—these characteristics of infants open our hearts to be in harmony with God's will for us.

Our trust has been broken. People have used us, abused us, abandoned us. It isn't our fault. We have no control over how others behave or think. Yet we do have the power to forgive, move on, and heal, and we must find the courage to trust ourselves again.

Many of us are afraid to be vulnerable. We worry that being vulnerable means opening ourselves to being hurt. Conscious vulnerability, however, is the humility to admit that we need God. We need God's love to nurture and guide us. We need God's strength to face life's challenges.

Many of us are certain our innocence is gone forever. We've been everywhere, done everything, become cynical and disillusioned. We feel used up and weary. Yet in our deepest heart space, our innocence is pure and untouched. We know and love God, and we know God knows and loves us.

With practice, we dare to trust again; we let go of pride and ask God to show us how to live; we make friends with our innocence and rejoice in the simplicity of our faith. This precious faith gives us the courage to place our lives into God's care, that we may be shown how to live God's will of love and forgiveness.

Ponder: Why am I afraid to trust?

Prayer: Lord, do not abandon me, for I am small and weak. I need your love.

Practice: Today I will be faithful by entrusting my heart's secret to God in prayer.

Thursday of the Fifteenth Week in Ordinary Time

YEAR I

Exodus 3:13–20
Psalm 105:1 and 5, 8–9, 24–25, 26–27

YEAR II

Isaiah 26:7–9, 12, 16–19
Psalm 102:13–14ab and 15, 16–18, 19–21

YEARS I AND II

Matthew 11:28–30

[Jesus said,] "Come to me, all you that are weary and are carrying heavy burdens, and I will give you rest."

MATTHEW 11:28

Reflection: Sometimes we just wear out. We are tired, spiritless, sad, and lacking in hope. We find it difficult to meet our daily obligations. We doubt we have a purpose. We wonder if life will always be bleak.

Sometimes we carry heavy burdens. We may have health or financial problems. We may be caring for elderly parents who are becoming more frail and forgetful every day. We may be in a dead-end job with no hope for advancement or a higher salary. We may not have a job and be unable to find one. We may be alienated from our family and feel the grief of having lost our roots. We may live in a community whose values are at odds with ours, and we feel alone and friendless. We may worry about terrorism, war, and slavery. We may view natural disasters such as tornadoes and tsunamis as signs that God is punishing the world.

Perhaps the heaviest burden we carry—and the thing that wears us out most—is thinking that we have to make sense of life. Yet we haven't been called to figure out life; we've been called to have faith in God's love and goodness. We've been called to entrust our thoughts, emotions, and actions to God. We've been called to surrender to God's will of love and mercy.

We've been called to come to Jesus, to turn to him in our weary and burdened state and be at rest in his heart of comfort and compassion.

Ponder: What burdens do I carry?

Prayer: Lord, you invite me to rest in you. Teach me to lay down my burdens and rest in the comfort of your love.

Practice: Today I will be faithful by resting from worry.

Friday of the Fifteenth Week in Ordinary Time

YEAR I
Exodus 11:10—12:14
Psalm 116:12–13, 15 and 16bc, 17–18

YEAR II
Isaiah 38:1–6, 21–22, 7–8
Psalm Isaiah 38:10, 11, 12abcd, 16

YEARS I AND II
Matthew 12:1–8

[Jesus said to them,] "But if you had known what this means, 'I desire mercy and not sacrifice", you would not have condemned the guiltless."

Matthew 12:7

Reflection: Whenever we struggle to make things happen—to force life to bend to our will—we need to take a step back. We need to admit our need for God and ask God for guidance. We need to open our minds and hearts to God's will. We need to be ready to move forward according to God's will. We need to remember that God wants us to move through life showing mercy to ourselves and others.

How do we ground our lives in mercy? We seek to understand ourselves and what motivates us. We uncover our hidden fears, prejudices, and resentments. We develop compassion for the parts of us that have been hurt, rejected, and neglected. We ask God to heal us from all that prevents us from loving ourselves and our neighbors.

This deep inner work begins to influence our interactions with others. We seek to understand what motivates others. We learn to identify the same types of fears, prejudices, and resentments that we have carried. We empathize with the hurts and wounds that others experience. We become interested in finding out what we have in common with others rather than condemning others for being different from us. We find that we're quicker to forgive, quicker to offer encouragement, and quicker to let go of negative judgment. We begin to feel a spacious sense of God's presence, and we know that God's mercy has touched our hearts and our lives and is making a difference.

Ponder: How do I express mercy in my interactions?

Prayer: Lord, you shower me with endless mercy and forgiveness. Help me to show mercy.

Practice: Today I will be faithful by intentionally choosing mercy over judgment in my thoughts, words, and actions.

Saturday of the Fifteenth Week in Ordinary Time

YEAR I
Exodus 12:37–42
Psalm 136:1 and 23–24, 10–12, 13–15

YEAR II
Micah 2:1–5
Psalm 10:1–2, 3–4, 7–8, 14

YEARS I AND II
Matthew 12:14–21

Many crowds followed [Jesus], and he cured all of them, and he ordered them not to make him known.

MATTHEW 12:15B

Reflection: We respond positively to people who make us feel good about ourselves. We're motivated by people who encourage and support our efforts to make changes. We're touched by people who show us love and compassion when we're suffering and in pain. We're inspired by people who demonstrate courage in challenging situations. We're inclined to follow people who are humble of heart and who do good things for others.

As we mix with people in our communities, at work, at meetings, and in public, we don't often think about how our thoughts, words, and actions influence others. We never know who is listening to us and watching us as we interact. We're unaware of the impact a kind word or a compassionate act might have. We're shocked when people tell us we made a difference. We find it unbelievable that others consider us to be a positive role model.

People of faith are inspired by Jesus' life, ministry, and teachings. We inspire others to believe in and follow Jesus by imitating the way Jesus welcomed strangers, forgave sinners, preached nonviolence, showed compassion to the poor, and lifted up the lowly. Discipleship is a way of life based on the gospel. We are called to give humble witness to the gospel in the crowds and inspire all people to follow Jesus.

Ponder: How do my actions and words influence people?

Prayer: Lord, your humble life and ministry is a model for humanity. Help me imitate your life and be a humble servant to all people.

Practice: Today I will be faithful by being selfless, loving, and humble in the presence of others.

Sixteenth Sunday in Ordinary Time

YEAR A

Wisdom 12:13, 16–19
Psalm 86:5–6, 9–10, 15–16
Romans 8:26–27
Matthew 13:24–43

[Jesus] told them another parable: "The kingdom of heaven is like yeast that a woman took and mixed in with three measures of flour until all of it was leavened."

MATTHEW 13:33

Reflection: We're cautious about how we involve ourselves in others' lives. We keep ourselves busy, leaving very little time to be with a family member, visit a neighbor, or write a note to a dear friend.

We look at life from a distance. We limit our involvement in the community because we don't want to complicate our lives. It's too messy to work with the poor and homeless, to visit someone in jail, to work with troubled youth, and to listen to stories of the abused. We don't get mixed up in situations that might bring more emotional and physical stress.

We underestimate the power of love expressed in simple ways. A simple hello, a written note, a short visit, a kind word, and a little support can change a person's outlook. The donation of pocket change, a few cans of food, and some items of clothing can help eliminate despair and poverty. Volunteering in the community promotes nonviolence and peace in our neighborhoods.

People of faith believe the kingdom of heaven is planted in our hearts. We understand that the kingdom of heaven is a life-changing force on earth. We manifest the kingdom of heaven in the environment through simple acts of love, compassion, forgiveness, and nonviolence. We show the power of our faith when we involve ourselves in the human condition.

Ponder: Where can I make a difference?

Prayer: Lord, you revealed the power of the kingdom of heaven on earth. Help me plant the seeds of love, compassion, and peace in the hearts of all people.

Practice: Today I will be faithful by making a donation to a charity.

YEAR B

Jeremiah 23:1–6
Psalm 23:1–3, 3–4, 5, 6
Ephesians 2:13–18
Mark 6:30–34

I will raise up shepherds over them who will shepherd them, and they shall not fear any longer, or be dismayed, nor shall any be missing, says the LORD.

JEREMIAH 23:4

Reflection: When we're anxious and fearful, we look for someone we can trust. When we're in need, we look for someone to help us. When we're sick, we look for someone to comfort us. When we're sad and depressed, we look for someone to support us. When we're lonely and rejected, we look for someone to love us. When we're hurt and suffering, we look for someone to show us compassion. When we're lost and confused, we look for someone to guide us.

We know from our own brokenness how important it is to have caring, supportive people to help us heal. We're aware that many people have prolonged mental anguish, emotional and physical abuse, poverty, disease, oppression, and violence and do not have the support of family, friends, and community.

When we become deaf to the cry of the poor and sick, indifferent to the plight of migrants and refugees, and unresponsive to abuse victims, people live in fear. When we do not let our pain and suffering inform us about the frailty of the human condition and move us to care for others, people perish.

People of faith believe we have been called by God to be shepherds of love and compassion. We feel a deep bond with the poor and suffering and a responsibility to care for them and work together to improve their lot.

Ponder: Whom do I rely on when I'm suffering?

Prayer: Lord, you are the Good Shepherd who cares for all people. Help me be a good shepherd of love and compassion.

Practice: Today I will be faithful by being a model of the Good Shepherd.

YEAR C

Genesis 18:1–10a
Psalm 15:2–3, 3–4, 5
Colossians 1:24–28
Luke 10:38–42

Now as they went on their way, [Jesus] entered a certain village, where a woman named Martha welcomed him into her home. She had a sister named Mary, who sat at the Lord's feet and listened to what he was saying.

LUKE 10:38–39

Reflection: Hospitality is an important aspect of life. It's at the heart of community. Hospitality is the way we show acceptance, love, and kindness to others. It's how we let them know we're not afraid to invite them into our lives. It is in the home that we first learn the meaning of hospitality and the importance of practicing discernment when inviting people into our lives. When we fail to practice hospitality, people become afraid and grow apart.

We live in a culture that controls us with messages of fear. We're conditioned to be afraid of strangers, especially people from different racial groups, ethnic backgrounds, and religious traditions. We're led to believe that terrorists are all around, waiting to destroy us and our way of life. We perpetuate a fear-of-others attitude with our inability to welcome strangers and undocumented immigrants, our uneasiness around the poor, and our unwillingness to volunteer in our community.

People of faith see the relationship between hospitality and prayer. Conditioned by the message of the gospel, we live and act out of love and compassion for others. We see hospitality as a response to God's presence and to the gospel's command to love our neighbor.

We can create communities of welcome by cultivating practices of hospitality and prayerful discernment. We can live in peace together when we see people not as our enemies but as our brothers and sisters.

Ponder: Who makes me feel afraid and unsafe?

Prayer: Lord, you teach us to love and welcome strangers. Remove the fear that keeps me from accepting and loving people with backgrounds different from mine.

Practice: Today I will be faithful by being nonjudgmental and accepting.

Monday of the Sixteenth Week in Ordinary Time

YEAR I
Exodus 14:5–18
Exodus 15:1–2, 3–4, 5–6

YEAR II
Micah 6:1–4, 6–8
Psalm 50:5–6, 8–9, 16bc–17, 21 and 23

YEARS I AND II
Matthew 12:38–42

"Teacher, we wish to see a sign from you."

MATTHEW 12:38

Reflection: We need words and actions to communicate. Our words and gestures give people insight into who we are; they're signs of our innermost thoughts and feelings. This is why it's so important to be as unambiguous as possible when speaking and acting. Although it's our nature to be good, we still struggle to discern what goodness is and appropriate ways to express this goodness.

Feeding the poor, building a home for the homeless, visiting the sick and the imprisoned, working with undocumented immigrants, and bringing supplies to people who have no access to food and water are signs of love and compassion. Speaking out against racism, discrimination, genocide, human trafficking, violence, and war is a sign of a person committed to justice and peace.

Walking past people in need, watching as people are bullied and physically abused, and failing to speak out in defense of life, human freedom, and peace are signs of indifference and uncaring toward the least of our brothers and sisters. Our inactivity and silence in the face of human tragedies exacerbate others' pain and suffering. Many people are suffering and in pain, looking for a sign that we care enough to speak out and do something on their behalf.

As people of faith, we understand that at baptism we were made children of the light, signs of God's goodness and love in the world. We are called to speak and embody God's Word, giving witness to the truth that we're made in God's image and likeness.

Ponder: What do my words and actions say about me?

Prayer: Lord, your words and deeds reveal the power of God. May my words and actions reveal your goodness and love.

Practice: Today I will be faithful by speaking and acting out of love.

Tuesday of the Sixteenth Week in Ordinary Time

YEAR I

Exodus 14:21–15:1
Exodus 15:8–9, 10, 12, 17

YEAR II

Micah 7:14–15, 18–20
Psalm 85:2–4, 5–6, 7–8

YEARS I AND II

Matthew 12:46–50

[Jesus] said, "For whoever does the will of my Father in heaven is my brother and sister and mother."

MATTHEW 12:50

Reflection: By our faith in Jesus, we seek to do the will of God by loving our neighbor, showing compassion to those in need, finding peaceful solutions to conflict, forgiving those who hurt us, and sharing our plenty with those who have nothing. By our faith in Jesus, we are the family of God. By our faith in Jesus, we are all sisters, brothers, mothers, and fathers to one another.

What kind of family are we as followers of Jesus? Are we a dysfunctional family? Do we have shameful secrets? Do some members dominate over others? Do some members do all the work? Are we afraid to let our voices be heard? Do we enjoy mealtimes together? Do we invite strangers to join us at the table? Do we love one another? Do we feel safe with one another? How do we relate to one another?

A family is a community that must reflect the love shared among God, Jesus, and the Holy Spirit. As the family of God, we must cultivate the God qualities of love, compassion, forgiveness, and mercy. As the family of God, we must learn to create relationships with all people everywhere. As the family of God, we must let go of prejudice and be willing to accept and love each other with all our individual quirks and eccentricities.

A human family will always be imperfect, but when we intentionally encourage each other to grow in holiness, we are moving in the direction of perfect love.

Ponder: How do I discern and do God's will?

Prayer: Lord, I surrender my life and will to you. Help me be a loving member of your family.

Practice: Today I will be faithful by treating all people with the respect due to members of God's family.

Wednesday of the Sixteenth Week in Ordinary Time

YEAR I
Exodus 16:1–5, 9–15
Psalm 78:18–19, 23–24, 25–26, 27–28

YEAR II
Jeremiah 1:1, 4–10
Psalm 71:1–2, 3–4a, 5–6ab, 15 and 17

YEARS I AND II
Matthew 13:1–9

"Let anyone with ears listen!"

MATTHEW 13:9

Reflection: We hear sounds of nature. We hear the sound of the wind, the rain falling, the birds singing, the animals running, the river flowing, the ocean waves crashing against the shore, and the tree branches swaying. We hear the sounds of the human condition. We hear babies crying, children playing, and people laughing. We hear the noises of the world. We hear cars, motorcycles, trucks and trains moving along, horns blasting, airplanes passing overhead, construction everywhere, bells tolling, phones ringing, and loud music.

In the midst of all the sounds and noises, we struggle to create moments of silence to listen to the longings of the human heart. Without silence we remain disconnected from ourselves and our environment; we have no capacity to search for the truth and the deeper meaning of our human existence. Because we are constantly distracted by noise, we cannot discern and interpret the signs of the times. We're muted to the quiet voices of people trapped in the deplorable conditions of poverty and human suffering. Without an attentive heart, we cannot feel their pain and respond with compassion.

As people of faith, we long to listen for the quiet voice of God beneath the sounds of nature and the noises of the world. We listen to the voice of God in Scripture and interpret the human condition in light of God's wisdom and truth. We imitate the life of Jesus, who prayerfully discerned and followed God's will. When we listen, we can know, love, and serve God and our neighbor faithfully.

Ponder: Why is it difficult for me to listen?

Prayer: Lord, you taught us how to pray and respond to the needs of all people. Give me an attentive heart, that I may respond compassionately to the needs of others.

Practice: Today I will be faithful by listening attentively for and responding to the cry of those in need.

Thursday of the Sixteenth Week in Ordinary Time

YEAR I
Exodus 19:1–2, 9–11, 16–20
Daniel 3:52, 53, 54, 55, 56

YEAR II
Jeremiah 2:1–3, 7–8, 12–13
Psalm 36:6–7ab, 8–9, 10–11

YEARS I AND II
Matthew 13:10–17

[Jesus answered,] "But blessed are your eyes, for they see, and your ears, for they hear."

MATTHEW 13:16

Reflection: How blessed we are to see with the eyes of faith. We see God's love in action everywhere we look. We see God's love in the harmony of science. We see God's love in the intricacies of our physical bodies. We see God's love in the changing seasons of the year, each with particular plants, insects, and animals following a delicate plan that keeps our world in balance.

We see God's love in the night sky, brilliant with stars and planets that move according to God's vision. We see God's love in the beautiful colors of the sunrise and sunset. We see God's love in the eyes of the people we love. We see God's love in the smile of a stranger. We see God's love in our helping hands.

How blessed are we to hear with ears of faith. We hear God's love in the whisper of the wind. We hear God's love in the surf. We hear God's love in bird song, farm sounds, and in the purrs and tail thumping of our pets. We hear God's love in the voices of our children. We hear God's love in the cries of those who are afraid, grieving, or poverty-stricken. We hear God's love in the silence of prayer.

Our faith calls us to see and hear God wherever we go. Our faith calls us to be mindful of God's presence in everything we do, in every person we encounter. Our faith calls us to be the eyes and ears of God in our fragile world.

Ponder: How does faith change the way I see and hear?

Prayer: Lord, you are the source of life. Open my eyes and ears to know you in every moment and in all of your precious human family.

Practice: Today I will be faithful by listening to the silence of God.

Friday of the Sixteenth Week in Ordinary Time

YEAR I

Exodus 20:1–17
Psalm 19:8, 9, 10, 11

YEAR II

Jeremiah 3:14–17
Jeremiah 31:10, 11–12abcd, 13

YEARS I AND II

Matthew 13:18–23

[Jesus answered,] "But as for what was sown on good soil, this is the one who hears the word and understands it, who indeed bears fruit and yields, in one case a hundredfold, in another sixty, and in another thirty."

MATTHEW 13:23

Reflection: The Word of God is the seed of love planted in our hearts. Our hearts are good soil.

Our hearts may have known sorrow, grief, or pain. Our hearts may be deeply wounded. Our hearts may bear the scars of broken trust, rejection, or abandonment. Yet our hearts remain good soil where the Word of God yields good fruit.

Our hearts may have closed against others out of fear or resentment. Our hearts may have hardened toward others because of anger or pride. Our hearts may be tortured from guilt or shame. Yet our hearts remain good soil where the Word of God yields good fruit.

We may feel we cannot trust our hearts because we've made unwise choices that have harmed ourselves and others. We may feel our hearts are unclean from the way we've conducted our lives. We may feel our hearts will never recover from a lifetime of self-abuse, self-hatred, and self-denial. Yet our hearts remain good soil where the Word of God yields good fruit.

The Word of God touches the sadness, shame, and wounds that have been part of our human experience. The Word of God gently opens the closed spaces of our hearts to feel the warmth and comfort of God's love. The Word of God works in our hearts to heal us from all that prevents us from loving ourselves and our neighbors.

Ponder: What prevents me from reading and understanding the Word of God?

Prayer: Lord, your Word consoles and gladdens me in my sorrow. Open my heart to welcome your Word that I may share your love and compassion with all my sisters and brothers.

Practice: Today I will be faithful by reading Matthew 13:18–23.

Saturday of the Sixteenth Week in Ordinary Time

YEAR I

Exodus 24:3–8
Psalm 50:1–2, 5–6, 14–15

YEAR II

Jeremiah 7:1–11
Psalm 84:3, 4, 5–6a and 8a, 11

YEARS I AND II

Matthew 13:24–30

[The householder] answered, "An enemy has done this."

MATTHEW 13:28

Reflection: How quick we are to see an enemy sabotaging our life, our family, our job, our schoolwork, our relationships. How quick we are to accuse others when situations seem unjust, threatening, or destructive. How quick we are to blame our failures, our broken promises, our disappointments, and our tragedies on someone else or on some outside factor.

Blaming others rarely solves anything. Blaming others is an angry reaction to a reality that may be upsetting, terrifying, or devastating. Blaming others causes division. Blaming others gives us the illusion of control, yet in reality it separates us from our heart, the foundation of our love and faith.

If, instead of blaming others, we take the time to look deeply at ourselves, we may find we're our own enemy. We've sown seeds of prejudice, intolerance, and spite. We've planted weeds of low self-esteem, insecurity, and doubt. We've cultivated hedgerows of resentment, bitterness, and disapproval. We've developed a wilderness of dissatisfaction, self-pity, and hopelessness.

As we look deeply into our hearts, we may be tempted to blame ourselves for being less than perfect. It's time to let go of our need to blame and become willing to accept the way we are—weaknesses, flaws, strengths, and gifts. With acceptance comes compassion. With compassion comes a deepening awareness of the love of God working in our hearts to transform us. In the light of God's love, we learn to trust that God is in charge and to change habits that keep us isolated and afraid. We find the faith to believe that all will be well.

Ponder: When am I my own worst enemy?

Prayer: Lord, you forgive me and accept me just as I am. Open my eyes to see the truth of your love in all situations.

Practice: Today I will be faithful by taking full responsibility for my actions.

Seventeenth Sunday
in Ordinary Time

YEAR A

1 Kings 3:5, 7–12
Psalm 119:57, 72, 76–77, 127–128, 129–130
Romans 8:28–30
Matthew 13:44–52

"Again, the kingdom of heaven is like a merchant in search of fine pearls; on finding one pearl of great value, he went and sold all that he had and bought it."

MATTHEW 13:45

Reflection: We value human life. It's our most precious gift. We know from personal experience how fragile life is and how important it is to protect life from mental, emotional, spiritual, and physical harm. We value family life. The family is the foundation of the society; without strong, stable families, children and youth are at risk. We value community life. We rely on our neighbors and friends to support us in times of trouble. We have come to discover that life, family, and community are the pearls of great value necessary for a happy life.

We live in a society where human life, family, and community aren't seen as precious gifts but as commodities to be controlled and manipulated by external forces. The secular world has no interest in the search for the meaning and purpose of life, no regard for the intrinsic dignity of the human person, and no interest in the common good. This is reflected in the endless search for instant gratification, the over-dependency on technology for a sense of belonging, and a growing lack of social responsibility.

As people of faith, we believe the kingdom of heaven is present and active in the earthly world. With the eyes of faith, we can see the kingdom of heaven buried in every life, in every family, and in our relationships with others. We do everything in our power to respond wholeheartedly to the presence of God's kingdom by defending life, showing respect to all people, being compassionate to the poor, and building a just and peaceful world.

Ponder: How do I cherish the pearls of life, family, and friends?

Prayer: Lord, you reveal the kingdom of heaven on earth. Help me be more aware of God's presence.

Practice: Today I will be faithful by spending quality time with a family member or friend.

YEAR B

2 Kings 4:42–44
Psalm 145:10–11, 15–16, 17–18
Ephesians 4:1–6
John 6:1–15

Then Jesus took the loaves, and when he had given thanks, he distributed them to those who were seated; so also the fish, as much as they wanted. When they were satisfied, he told his disciples, "Gather up the fragments left over, so that nothing may be lost."

JOHN 6:11–12

Reflection: We have more than we need to live a comfortable life. We're not always careful about what we buy. We don't always discern how people's lives are impacted by what we buy for ourselves.

When we prepare a meal at home, we usually have more than enough food to eat. We keep the leftovers for another meal or throw them away. When we go to a restaurant, there is usually more than enough food to eat. We take the leftovers home or leave them for the garbage. We don't think about what leftovers mean in a world in which people are starving. Our leftovers could save millions of lives.

Think about the water we use to bathe and clean our vehicles. We're not concerned about the people living in drought-stricken areas where there is no water to drink. Think about the shoes and clothes we own but hardly wear. We dress ourselves each day mindless of the people who have no clothing and shelter. We keep extra change in the car for the parking meter, but we're not diligent about setting aside extra change for the poor and needy.

As people of faith, we've been taught by Jesus to feed the poor, clothe the naked, and shelter the homeless. We're challenged by the gospel to overcome our selfishness and become selfless servants of love and compassion.

Ponder: How can I downsize and simplify my life?

Prayer: Lord, you are the bread that satisfies hungry hearts. Remove the selfishness from my heart, that I may be generous to people in need.

Practice: Today I will be faithful by cleaning out my closet and donating items to charity.

YEAR C

Genesis 18:20–32
Psalm 138:1–2, 2–3, 6–7, 7–8
Colossians 2:12–14
Luke 11:1–13

"And forgive us our sins, for we ourselves forgive everyone indebted to us."

LUKE 11:4A

Reflection: We're familiar with the burden of financial debt. We're indebted to banks or other lending institutions that lend us money to finance a home, a car, or a college education. If we default on our loans, they're usually not so forgiving; they penalize us for being late. Financial institutions aren't in the business of releasing people from their debts.

Just like the financial institutions, we keep account of painful experiences and memories. We find it difficult to show tenderness to people who called us terrible names, misrepresented us, abused us, and slandered us. We still carry deep anger for people who took advantage of our goodness, betrayed our friendship, and rejected us. We're too prideful to mend broken relationships and be reconciled with family and friends. We keep blaming others for our chronic unhappiness and dissatisfaction.

People of faith believe Jesus came to offer love and forgiveness to all people. We know we can't forgive others on our own. First, we need to experience the power of God's loving forgiveness before we're able to offer it to others. Our willingness to forgive helps us live in right relationship with God and neighbor. The gospel teaches us that we have access to God's forgiveness through prayer. As we pray for God's forgiveness, we're empowered to forgive everyone indebted to us.

Ponder: Whom do I find it difficult to forgive?

Prayer: Lord, you came to offer God's forgiveness to all people. Help me forgive my brothers and sisters from the heart.

Practice: Today I will be faithful by forgiving someone I've held a grudge against for a while.

Monday of the Seventeenth Week in Ordinary Time

YEAR I
Exodus 32:15–24, 30–34
Psalm 106:19–20, 21–22, 23

YEAR II
Jeremiah 13:1–11
Psalm DEUTERONOMY *32:18–19, 20, 21*

YEARS I AND II
Matthew 13:31–35

"It is the smallest of all the seeds, but when it has grown it is the greatest of shrubs and becomes a tree, so that the birds of the air come and make nests in its branches."

MATTHEW 13:32

Reflection: In each of us is the seed of God's Spirit, giving us the potential to grow in compassion, love, peace, and unity until others find refuge, rest, and comfort in our presence.

God's Spirit nestles in our heart space. Whatever happens during our lifetimes, God's Spirit sustains us, calls us, nurtures us, and challenges us. Whether or not we're aware of God's Spirit, it supports us through the intricacies of life.

Whenever we take the time to be present to another person; whenever we respond to anger with kindness; whenever we choose forgiveness over resentment; whenever we pray to be shown God's will; whenever we seek to know God more intimately through study of Scripture or meditation on the Word; whenever we widen our awareness of the needs of the poor, neglected, abused, abandoned, or marginalized; whenever we share generously with those in need—we are guided by the Spirit.

We don't have to be famous, rich, or glamorous to grow spiritually. All we need is the willingness to be guided by God's Spirit of infinite goodness. All we need is trust in God's Spirit of abundant love. All we need is faith in ourselves as beloved children of God, given a precious lifetime to manifest our goodness and love to all those we encounter.

Ponder: When do I recognize the work of God's Spirit within me?

Prayer: Lord, your Spirit lives deep within me. Help me let your love and compassion grow in me so that I may be a comfort to those in need.

Practice: Today I will be faithful by visiting and spending time with someone who is hurting.

Tuesday of the Seventeenth Week in Ordinary Time

YEAR I

Exodus 33:7–11, 34:5–9, 28
Psalm 103:6–7, 8–9, 10–11, 12–13

YEAR II

Jeremiah 14:17–22
Psalm 79:8, 9, 11 and 13

YEARS I AND II

Matthew 13:35–43

[Jesus] answered, "The one who sows the good seed is the Son of Man; the field is the world, and the good seed are the children of the kingdom; the weeds are the children of the evil one, and the enemy who sowed them is the devil."

MATTHEW 13:37–39A

Reflection: We learn the difference between right and wrong. We're taught to do what is right and avoid what is wrong. The good life is characterized by doing the right thing for the right reasons.

As we mature, we discover it's more difficult to discern right from wrong. Life isn't black and white, but a complex gray mix of competing philosophies, thoughts, ideas, and values. We struggle to find a clear vision, a single voice, and positive direction.

Perhaps our greatest challenge is surrounding ourselves with people grounded in a sense of the good who are deeply concerned about our well-being and the well-being of others. Having good people in our company helps us discern complex issues; good people give us clarity of thought, feeling, and life direction.

People of faith are guided by Jesus' life and teachings. We tend to trust people who build up life. We open our hearts to people who show compassion to the vulnerable. We listen attentively to people who speak from a vision of universal love and peace. We are inclined to follow people who are selfless in what they do for others.

Ponder: Who influences my life?

Prayer: Lord, you came to sow God's kingdom in the earthly world. Help me plant your seeds of forgiveness, love, and peace in the hearts of all people.

Practice: Today I will be faithful by being patient and kind.

Wednesday of the Seventeenth Week in Ordinary Time

YEAR I

Exodus 34:29–35
Psalm 99:5, 6, 7, 9

YEAR II

Jeremiah 15:10, 16–21
Psalm 59:2–3, 4, 10–11, 17, 18

YEARS I AND II

Matthew 13:44–46

> "Again, the kingdom of heaven is like a merchant in search of fine pearls; on finding one pearl of great value, he went and sold all that he had and bought it."

MATTHEW 13:45–46

Reflection: We're all searching. Sometimes we try to name what we're searching for: the perfect job, the right life, success, wealth, serenity, sobriety, health, affirmation, friendship, companionship, love. We search because something deep inside pushes us. Our real search is for God.

We all long to be one with God. Even if we think we don't believe in God, our deepest longing is for God. We long to be at rest and at peace in God's loving, forgiving, accepting embrace. We long for the loving heart of God to heal all our fears, disappointments, and grief. We long for the courage and grace to look at God and know we're loved beyond understanding.

The Spirit of God deep within us pushes us to open our minds, eyes, ears, and hearts to find God. We need to look beyond our human failings, beyond the personality quirks and flaws, beyond the physical façade—and glimpse the magnificence of who we are: precious children of God made in love and in God's image of love and goodness.

This magnificence is the pearl of great value that has been placed in our hearts. This is the pearl we must search for. This is the pearl we must respect and cherish not only in ourselves, but also in all members of God's precious human family.

Ponder: What prevents me from believing I'm a magnificent child of God?

Prayer: Lord, I long to be in your presence. Help me keep searching to find the kingdom of heaven in my heart.

Practice: Today I will be faithful by intentionally remembering God when I look in the mirror.

Thursday of the Seventeenth Week in Ordinary Time

YEAR I
Exodus 40:16–21, 34–38
Psalm 84:3, 4, 5–6, 8, 11

YEAR II
Jeremiah 18:1–6
Psalm 146:1b–2, 3–4, 5–6ab

YEARS I AND II
Matthew 13:47–53

"Again, the kingdom of heaven is like a net that was thrown into the sea and caught fish of every kind; when it was full, they drew it ashore, sat down, and put the good into baskets but threw out the bad."

MATTHEW 13:47–48

Reflection: Each human life has the potential to reflect the kingdom of heaven—the place of love, forgiveness, peace, and unity that welcomes all people without exception.

Yet when we throw a net into our experiences, we find it catches a lot more than love, forgiveness, peace, and unity. Our net holds the *all* of our life, the positive and negative. Our challenge is to sort through the net and decide what we need to discard and what we need to keep.

We can discard old feelings of resentment, anger, and bitterness. We can discard prejudice, indifference, and disdain. We can discard greed, arrogance, and envy. We can discard gossip, jealousy, and mean-spiritedness. We can discard sarcasm, criticism, and acrimony. We can discard low self-esteem, despair, and hopelessness.

We need to keep kindness, respect, and courtesy. We need to keep joy, humor, and playfulness. We need to keep wonder, curiosity, and creativity. We need to keep humility, vulnerability, and gentleness. We need to keep generosity, sensitivity, and compassion. We need to keep love, faith, and willingness to rely on God's gracious guidance.

As we discern what to discard and what to keep in our experience net, we find that our lives become lighter and more manageable, reflecting more perfectly the kingdom of heaven.

Ponder: What experiences must I discard and keep?

Prayer: Lord, you bless me with all that is good. Help me discern the attitudes and behaviors I need to discard.

Practice: Today I will be faithful by going through my home and donating items I don't need to an organization that will use them to benefit the poor and needy.

Friday of the Seventeenth Week in Ordinary Time

YEAR I

Leviticus 23:1, 4–11, 15–16, 34–37
Psalm 81:3–4, 5–6, 10–11

YEAR II

Jeremiah 26:1–9
Psalm 69:5, 8–10, 14

YEARS I AND II

Matthew 13:54–58

And [Jesus] did not do many deeds of power there, because of their unbelief.

MATTHEW 13:58

Reflection: Faith is a gift. When we have it, we believe without understanding. We love without hesitation. We accept without doubt. We enjoy the moment without worry about the future. We live in the present without regretting the past. We make plans but don't plan outcomes. We put our lives into God's loving care, and we trust that all is well.

Sometimes we live our faith easily. We go with the moment. We let go of control and manipulation. We accept kindness, encouragement, and love. We see God's love and goodness in people, in the beauty of nature, in the companionship of our pets. We deal with hardship and grief without despair or self-pity.

At other times, it's a struggle to live a faith-filled life. We feel overburdened by responsibilities, illness, or financial obligations. We wonder why God isn't working miracles in our lives. We doubt our own goodness. We lose heart when we hear of cruelty, terrorism, slavery, war, and abuse. We feel forgotten and alienated from our center, our source—our God.

Faith is a gift we must nurture. When we feel God has forgotten us, we can practice believing God is listening. When we wonder where the miracles are, we can deliberately look at a sunrise or sunset and practice believing God made a painting just for us. When we feel overburdened, we can get on our knees, ask God to help us, and practice believing that God has answered.

Ponder: What causes me doubt and confusion?

Prayer: Lord, in your great love, answer me. Heal my unbelief. Increase my faith in your love and care for myself and for my sisters and brothers.

Practice: Today I will be faithful by believing God loves me.

Saturday of the Seventeenth Week in Ordinary Time

YEAR I

Leviticus 25:1, 8–17
Psalm 67:2–3, 5, 7–8

YEAR II

Jeremiah 26:11–16, 24
Psalm 69:15–16, 30–31, 33–34

YEARS I AND II

Matthew 14:1–12

But when Herod's birthday came, the daughter of Herodias danced before the company, and she pleased Herod so much that he promised on oath to grant her whatever she might ask.

MATTHEW 14:6–7

Reflection: King Herod made a commitment that caused the death of John the Baptist. He didn't take time to consider the consequences of his blanket promise to Herodias' daughter.

Sometimes we, too, make commitments without taking the time to consider: Do I have time for this? Do I have the energy for this? Do I have the talent for this? Do I want to do this? How will this commitment affect my life and the lives of those around me?

Commitments are part of life. We commit ourselves to love and take care of our families. We commit ourselves to our work or studies. We commit ourselves to a community, to give and receive support. These are commitments that help us live responsible, fulfilled lives.

We have other commitments too. We sign up to coach volleyball, softball, and youth basketball. We serve on boards. We volunteer at soup kitchens, hospitals, and nursing homes. We deliver items to food pantries. We participate in walks that raise money to fund research on cancer, diabetes, and Alzheimer's disease.

Perhaps the most important commitment we make is to our faith. We actively commit to our faith when we meditate on sacred Scripture, spend time in prayer, and seek quiet moments where we listen for God's guidance. These spiritual practices underline our commitment to be guided by God's will—and this is the only commitment we must make to grow in our likeness to God's love and goodness.

Ponder: What is the nature of my commitments?

Prayer: Lord, your face shines on me in love and acceptance. Help me keep my commitment to love you and my neighbor.

Practice: Today I will be faithful by taking time to pray before making commitments.

Eighteenth Sunday in Ordinary Time

YEAR A

Isaiah 55:1–3
Psalm 145:8–9, 15–16, 17–18
Romans 8:35, 37–39
Matthew 14:13–21

Who will separate us from the love of Christ? Will hardship, or distress, or persecution, or famine, or nakedness, or peril, or sword?

ROMANS 8:35

Reflection: Along the spectrum of life, we experience hardship, pain, and distress. We deal with personal struggles, family issues, and social problems. The pressures of life overpower us, making us feel insecure, unstable, and vulnerable. Situations arise where we have no mental, emotional, spiritual, or physical strength. In the midst of troubles, we look for someone to love and support us.

Life isn't an easy road. Life isn't easy for the poor and homeless. Life is painful for those with cancer. Life is unbearable for those with mental illness. Life is a burden for the addicted. Life is a hardship for the unemployed. Life is a struggle for the divorced and separated. Life is fragile for those with HIV/AIDS. Life is dangerous for refugees. Life is cruel for the abused. Life is lonely for the arrogant. The human condition of brokenness and alienation provokes us to love and care for others.

People of faith believe life is protected and held together in Christ's love. We trust that no circumstance, no disaster, and no power will ever separate us from this love. The reassuring presence of Christ's love restores our hope; it strengthens us to continue the journey of life. We are called to be Christ's messengers of hope and peace to anyone who is suffering.

Ponder: What separates me from the love of God?

Prayer: Lord, your love and compassion are always with us in times of trouble. Help me walk in solidarity with those who are suffering and show them your love and compassion.

Practice: Today I will be faithful by being present to someone who is in pain.

YEAR B

Exodus 16:2–4, 12–15
Psalm 78:3–4, 23–24, 25, 54
Ephesians 4:17, 20–24
John 6:24–35

Jesus said to them, "I am the bread of life. Whoever comes to me will never be hungry, and whoever believes in me will never be thirsty."

JOHN 6:35

Reflection: Social media is a powerful influence. It shapes our thoughts and creates our perceptions. For some people, social media is the bread that can satisfy all our needs.

We have a hunger and thirst to be connected to people and know everything about them. We also have a hunger and thirst to be known through social networking. We share our personal story and the details of our experiences, yet we feel exposed and vulnerable. We hunger and thirst for intimacy. We go online to connect to virtual friends and form virtual relationships, but we're still lonely and unfulfilled.

We have a need to care. Social media draws us into people's lives; we become enmeshed in their struggles. We feed off their pain because it satisfies our need to be needed, but our need to be loved is never satisfied. We need to pay attention to how we allow social media to feed our inner longings.

People of faith believe God's Word is the source and foundation of our lives. We must be careful about the ways we satisfy our inner hunger and thirst. God's Word is the bread that satisfies our inner longing for happiness and peace. When we read and meditate on God's Word, we nourish the mind and heart with love, compassion, forgiveness, and peace. Being connected to God's Word helps us live in intimate relationship with God and neighbor.

Ponder: How do I satisfy my inner hunger and thirst?

Prayer: Lord, you are the bread of love, compassion, and peace. Strengthen me with this bread so I can serve others.

Practice: Today I will be faithful by reading and meditating on John 6:24–35.

YEAR C

Ecclesiastes 1:2; 2:21–23
Psalm 90:3–4, 5–6, 12–13, 14, 17
Colossians 3:1–5, 9–11
Luke 12:13–21

And [Jesus] said to them, "Take care! Be on your guard against all kinds of greed; for one's life does not consist in the abundance of possessions."

LUKE 12:15

Reflection: We can't deny the presence of greed. We see the face of greed whenever we're not satisfied with what we have and when the desire for more overwhelms our sensibilities. We struggle to keep our desire for more wealth, possessions, and power under control. We try to remind ourselves that money and possessions don't make us happy. They can be a burden and bring deep anxiety.

Yet we live in a culture that advocates a doctrine of greed. We see this doctrine in people who constantly think only of themselves, seeking instant gratification wherever they can find it. We see it played out in the lives of ruthless leaders who want more power and control. We're victims of the greedy schemes designed by financial institutions to become richer and more powerful. We cannot escape the social media and marketplace messages that convince us we need more things to make us happy.

People of faith must avoid all forms of greed, because greed is another name for idolatry. We believe God is the centerpiece of our lives, the source and foundation of our happiness on earth. We know that growing rich in what matters to God is better than growing rich in the things of the world. We become greedy when God is replaced by wealth, possessions, and power. We are called to grow rich in love, compassion, and peace.

Ponder: How do I deal with greed?

Prayer: Lord, you are the source and foundation of life. Help me grow rich in love and forgiveness as I share what I have with others.

Practice: Today I will be faithful by paying attention to spiritual matters rather than material things.

Monday of the Eighteenth Week in Ordinary Time

YEAR I
Numbers 11:4–15
Psalm 81:12–13, 14–15, 16–17

YEAR II
Jeremiah 28:1–17
Psalm 119:29, 43, 79, 80, 95, 102

YEARS I AND II
Matthew 14:13–21

Jesus said to them, "They need not go away; you give them something to eat."

MATTHEW 14:16

Reflection: Jesus shows us that however little we have, we always have enough to share with someone in need. We can spare a dollar. We can do without a new pair of jeans. We can donate from our cupboard to the food pantry. Everything we have is a gift from God. It's our responsibility to share our gifts—and not send those in need away with nothing.

It's not only money, clothing, food, or other concrete items that we're called to give. Sometimes we're called to give our wisdom and experience. Sometimes we're called to give our faith and hope in God's love. Sometimes we're called to give our knowledge and expertise.

Sometimes we're called to be patient when we feel impatient. Sometimes we're called to pay attention when we feel indifferent. Sometimes we're called to listen when we want to talk. Sometimes we're called to forgive when we want to hold on to resentment. Sometimes we're called to admit we're wrong when we want to be right. Sometimes we're called to visit an elderly relative when we want to stay quietly at home. Sometimes we're called to let others make their own choices when we want to control them.

Our call to be like Jesus opens our eyes, minds, and hearts to others' needs. As we grow to be more like Jesus, we intentionally choose to feed those we meet generously and with kindness, respect, compassion, and love.

Ponder: What do I have to share?

Prayer: Lord, teach me your ways. Help me share what I've been given with those in need.

Practice: Today I will be faithful by giving a little extra to those in need even if I feel I have nothing left to give.

Tuesday of the Eighteenth Week in Ordinary Time

YEAR I

Numbers 12:1–13
Psalm 51:3–4, 5–6, 6–7, 12–13

YEAR II

Jeremiah 30:1–2, 12–15, 18–22
Psalm 102:16–18, 19–21, 29, 22–23

YEARS I AND II

Matthew 14:22–36

But when [Peter] noticed the strong wind, he became frightened, and beginning to sink, he cried out, "Lord, save me!" Jesus immediately reached out his hand and caught him, saying to him, "You of little faith, why did you doubt?"

MATTHEW 14:30–31

Reflection: Sometimes we feel like we're walking on water. We're in tune with God's will; we love our neighbor as ourselves; we eat healthy foods, get enough sleep, and make time for recreation, work, prayer, and meditation. We offer comfort to the discouraged and sad, keep in touch with the lonely, and give generously to those in need. We have faith in God's nearness, in God's love, and in God's personal attention.

Other times we feel like we're sinking. We worry about finances. We're afraid no one loves us. We lose sleep over family members. We find it difficult to make decisions. We obsess about our health. We're anxious about the state of the world. Our doubts and fears make it difficult for us to believe that God is near, that God is taking care of us, that God loves us unconditionally.

When doubt and fear distort our thinking and way of living, it's time for us to cry out to the Lord to save us. Jesus will immediately lead us to serenity. We may need to cry out for help often during stressful times, letting go of our need to be strong and independent. As we experience God's nearness and saving love, we learn to live more fully in faith.

Ponder: When do I cry out for help?

Prayer: Lord, you are our God, and we are your people. Increase my faith in your love and goodness, that I may not be overtaken by fear and doubt.

Practice: Today I will be faithful by saying a prayer when I feel afraid or doubtful.

Wednesday of the Eighteenth Week in Ordinary Time

YEAR I
Numbers 13:1–2, 25–14:1, 26–29, 34–35
Psalm 106:6–7, 13–14, 21–22, 23

YEAR II
Jeremiah 31:1–7
Psalm Jeremiah 31:10, 11–12ab, 13

YEARS I AND II
Matthew 15:21–28

Jesus left that place and went away to the district of Tyre and Sidon. Just then a Canaanite woman from that region came out and started shouting, "Have mercy on me, Lord, Son of David; my daughter is tormented by a demon."

MATTHEW 15:21–22

Reflection: We relate well with people we've come to know over time. We feel comfortable with people who wear our skin, speak our language, and live in the same community. We don't fear greeting our neighbors on the street, working with them on a project, or talking with them at a social event. We offer our friends assistance and support in time of need. We welcome the opportunity to strengthen relationships with our neighbors and friends.

On the other hand, we may feel uneasy around people we don't know. We're uncomfortable with people who don't wear our skin or speak our language or live in our community. We fear greeting a stranger on the street, working next to a woman from a different country, standing next to a man from another religious tradition, socializing with a gay person. We're reluctant to welcome and offer help to anyone we perceive to threaten our comfort zone.

People of faith believe that every person is created in God's image and likeness. Our relationship with others is grounded in this truth. We also uphold the principle that every person is blessed with human dignity. This principle influences our thoughts, attitude, and behavior. With the healing power of God's love and compassion, we can liberate people tormented by the demons of hatred and discrimination.

Ponder: Who makes me feel uncomfortable?

Prayer: Lord, your love and compassion bring healing to all people. Help me trust in your love and care.

Practice: Today I will be faithful by being kind to all people.

Thursday of the Eighteenth Week in Ordinary Time

YEAR I

Numbers 20:1–13
Psalm 95:1–2, 6–7, 8–9

YEAR II

Jeremiah 31:31–34
Psalm 51:12–13, 14–15, 18–19

YEARS I AND II

Matthew 16:13–23

[Jesus] said to them, "But who do you say that I am?"

MATTHEW 16:15

Reflection: We are. We live, breathe, smile, laugh, cry, dance, walk, sleep, think, feel, hate, love. God has made us, and we are. We are God's. We are God's children. We are God's human family. We are in God, and God is in us.

We are God's eyes and ears and hands and heart. We are God's creation and creativity. We are God's forgiveness and mercy. We are God's peace and harmony. We are God's kindness and tenderness. We are God's gentleness and comfort. We are God's humor and joy. We are God's healing touch and encouraging presence. We are God's unconditional love and unfailing compassion.

We are Jesus' sisters and brothers. We are with Jesus in his mission to announce the Good News of God's unconditional love. We are with Jesus in his shame and suffering. We are with Jesus in the pain of his death. We are with Jesus in the joy of his resurrection. We are with Jesus in his obedience to God's will to love and serve each other without exception.

We are temples of God's Spirit. We are in the Spirit and with the Spirit. We are one with the Spirit in love and goodness. We are led by the Spirit, moved by the Spirit, touched by the Spirit, inspired by the Spirit.

Like Jesus, we ask, "Who am I?" Like Jesus, we know we are in the unity of God. Like Jesus, we know we are called to be faithful witnesses of God's love and compassion. Like Jesus, we know we cannot allow worldly distractions, others' opinions, or our own human frailty to deter us from our spiritual path.

Ponder: Who am I?

Prayer: Lord, you made us and we are yours. Create a clean heart in me that I may rejoice always in being your creation.

Practice: Today I will be faithful by remembering who I am.

Friday of the Eighteenth Week in Ordinary Time

YEAR I
Deuteronomy 4:32–40
Psalm 77:12–13, 14–15, 16, 21

YEAR II
Nahum 2:1, 3; 3:1–3, 6–7
Deuteronomy 32:35cd–36ab, 39abcd, 41

YEARS I AND II
Matthew 16:24–28

Then Jesus told his disciples, "If any want to become my followers, let them deny themselves and take up their cross and follow me."

MATTHEW 16:24

Reflection: Each day we are made aware of the mental, emotional, spiritual, and physical burdens of life. We know people who struggle with job loss, chronic illness, depression, and addiction. We support friends dealing with separation and divorce. We listen to colleagues weighed down by grief, fear, trauma, and anxiety. We admire people who face the burdens of life with courage. We do whatever we can to help others bear their load.

In helping others carry their burdens, we often overlook our own. We're afraid to admit we're weighed down by personal matters. We don't want people to know we carry secrets, painful memories, old wounds, and emotional baggage. We mask negative thoughts and feelings about ourselves and others. We're burdened by overwhelming shame, guilt, anger, jealousy, and resentment. We're exhausted from pretending that our life is burden free.

People of faith see struggles and burdens as graced opportunities to reflect on the mystery of the death and resurrection of Jesus. Jesus' cross teaches us that suffering has a deeper purpose and meaning in God's plan. We can carry our burdens knowing they don't diminish life, but strengthen our faith and hope in the promise of eternal life with God.

Ponder: What cross do I carry?

Prayer: Lord, by your cross and resurrection you redeemed the world. Help me inspire others as I bear struggles and burdens with trust and humility.

Practice: Today I will be faithful by bearing my burden without complaint.

Saturday of the Eighteenth Week in Ordinary Time

YEAR I
Deuteronomy 6:4–13
Psalm 18:2–3, 3–4, 47, 51

YEAR II
Habakkuk 1:12—2:4
Psalm 9:8–9, 10–11, 12–13

YEARS I AND II
Matthew 17:14–20

"For truly I tell you, if you have faith the size of a mustard seed, you will say to this mountain, 'Move from here to there', and it will move; and nothing will be impossible for you."

MATTHEW 17:20

Reflection: Just a tiny bit of faith is all we need. Just a morsel of belief in God's goodness and love. Just a crumb of reliance on God's mercy and forgiveness. Just a speck of conviction that we are beloved of God—precious, wanted, and a joy.

Faith is rooted in love. When we feel loved, we feel confident and secure. We feel we have a place in the world, that our lives have meaning, and that our presence matters. We feel powerful, humble, and grateful.

When we don't feel loved, we feel shaky and uncertain. We worry that we have no purpose. We feel lost and without direction. We may still pray, go to Mass, and read sacred Scripture, but we're not sure God cares about us.

We can intentionally cultivate faith by treating ourselves with love. We can speak kindly to ourselves. We can praise ourselves for a job well done. We can be mindful of our many gifts and talents and rejoice in sharing them. We can acknowledge our weaknesses and accept ourselves. We can practice gratitude for all we are and all we have. We can ask God to help us feel and accept God's love, peace, and compassion.

Faith is a gift, the fruit of love. When we live in, by, and through God's love, nothing is impossible.

Ponder: How reliable is my faith?

Prayer: Lord, you welcome us as we seek you. Open my heart to your love, that I may have complete faith in your compassion and mercy.

Practice: Today I will be faithful by asking God to surround and fill me with love.

Nineteenth Sunday
in Ordinary Time

YEAR A

1 Kings 19:9a, 11–13a
Psalm 85:9, 10, 11–12, 13–14
Romans 9:1–5
Matthew 14:22–33

**And after [Jesus] had dismissed the crowds,
he went up the mountain by himself to pray.
When evening came, he was there alone.**

MATTHEW 14:23

Reflection: When we were children, we had to be on good behavior. When we didn't behave as instructed, our parents made us take a time-out—go to our room or another designated place to think about what we'd done. We couldn't leave time-out until we promised to adjust our attitude and behavior. Time-out was also imposed when we were playing too roughly with siblings or friends. This was a good way to make sure we didn't end up hurting anyone.

Now that we're older, our lives are hectic and busy. Our behavior is out of control because we're overscheduled, overworked, and overwhelmed. We spend too much time driving from place to place, working, doing errands, completing unfinished projects, and attending social events. In between all these activities, we're surfing the Internet, reading and answering texts and e-mails, and checking social media.

We need to reclaim our childhood practice of taking time-outs. We need space to think about what we're doing and make changes.

People of faith learn from Jesus how to live the spiritual life. We know we can't live a meaningful, spiritual life without prayer. We need solitude to rest from work and other activities that distract us from being with God. We need time-outs from our busy lives to pray and reflect. We need long periods of rest to renew the mind, heart, soul, and body.

Ponder: When do I take time-outs to pray?

Prayer: Lord, you taught your disciples to pray. Help me cultivate the practices of prayer, fasting, and almsgiving.

Practice: Today I will be faithful by taking a time-out for solitude and prayer.

YEAR B

1 Kings 19:4–8
Psalm 34:2–3, 4–5, 6–7, 8–9
Ephesians 4:30—5:2
John 6:41–51

And do not grieve the Holy Spirit of God, with which you were marked with a seal for the day of redemption. Put away from you all bitterness and wrath and anger and wrangling and slander, together with all malice, and be kind to one another, tenderhearted, forgiving one another, as God in Christ has forgiven you.

EPHESIANS 4:30–32

Reflection: We've been the victims of demeaning, inappropriate behavior. We've been hurt deeply. We can catalog the times we were undermined, prejudged, ridiculed, mocked, discriminated against, misrepresented, misunderstood, rejected, and completely ignored. We carry painful memories of being attacked. We struggle each day to recover from mental and emotional wounds.

We can never condone mistreatment of others for any reason. We must refrain from participating in the destruction of another person's life and reputation. We must oppose physical abuse, bullying, rape, slavery, human trafficking, genocide, ethnic violence, and war. We have a duty and responsibility to cleanse the world of anything that threatens life.

People of faith believe the Holy Spirit makes us children of God. We live under the power and influence of the Spirit of God. The Spirit helps us examine our life, purifying our mind and heart. The Spirit empowers us to be kind, compassionate, loving, and forgiving. When we walk in the Spirit of God, we don't hurt others. Our words and actions build up people's lives, heal broken hearts, restore hope, and bring peace.

Ponder: When have my words and actions offended others?

Prayer: Lord, you give us your Spirit to renew the earth. Instill in my heart the spirit of love, compassion, forgiveness, and peace, that I may be a source of healing.

Practice: Today I will be faithful by making an examination of conscience before I go to bed.

YEAR C

Wisdom 18:6–9
Psalm 33:1, 12, 18–19, 20–22
Hebrews 11:1–2, 8–19
Luke 12:32–48

"Sell your possessions, and give alms. Make purses for yourselves that do not wear out, an unfailing treasure in heaven, where no thief comes near and no moth destroys. For where your treasure is, there your heart will be also."

LUKE 12:33–34

Reflection: We treasure our family. We will do everything in our power to preserve our relationship with members of our family. We treasure our friends. We will do anything to preserve the special bond we have with our friends. We treasure the community in which we live. We will join a neighborhood watch group to keep our community safe and secure. We treasure our possessions because they have special meaning. We will keep them in a safe place. For where our treasure is, there our heart will be also.

Our treasures aren't equal. Our possessions aren't more valuable than family and friends. Our possessions aren't more valuable than the poor child living in another neighborhood, the homeless veteran standing on a street corner, the incarcerated woman at the county jail, the gay teenager bullied at school, the lonely elderly person fading away at the nursing home, the undocumented immigrant looking for a job, and the frightened refugee begging for asylum. We sometimes forget that people, regardless of their condition and background, are more valuable than possessions.

People of faith are commanded to love God and neighbor. Our treasure is the unbreakable bond of love between God and humanity. We're called to be stewards of humanity, to care for the poor and the vulnerable. We treasure people from all walks of life because we believe God is the treasure intimately connected to the human condition.

Ponder: What is my heart's treasure?

Prayer: Lord, you offered your life out of love for humankind. Help me let go of my possessions so I can generously serve others.

Practice: Today I will be faithful by reexamining my priorities.

Monday of the Nineteenth Week in Ordinary Time

YEAR I

Deuteronomy 10:12–22
Psalm 147:12–13, 14–15, 19–20

YEAR II

Ezekiel 1:2–5, 24–28c
Psalm 148:1–2, 11–12, 13, 14

YEARS I AND II

Matthew 17:22–27

As they were gathering in Galilee, Jesus said to them, "The Son of Man is going to be betrayed into human hands, and they will kill him, and on the third day he will be raised." And they were greatly distressed.

MATTHEW 17:22–23

Reflection: We're often caught off-guard by breaking news. We're distressed to learn a family member has a terminal illness. We're shocked to be told a friend is getting a divorce. We're upset to hear a neighbor has had a miscarriage. We cry when a classmate is fatally wounded in the line of duty. We have difficulty coping with life's sudden twists and turns.

We can't predict our own future, but experience tells us that pain and suffering can't be avoided.

We will face personal heartache, disappointment, failure, illness, and trials. We can't foresee world events, but tragedies and natural disasters will take place. We will wake up to the sad news of nations at war, innocent people being falsely accused by brutal dictators, children dying from malnutrition and disease, young people being sold into human trafficking, and refugees seeking a new homeland.

People of faith don't deny disturbing and painful realities. We interpret them in light of Jesus' suffering, death, and resurrection. We endure unexpected challenges and problems because we're comforted by the goodness of others and have hope in the promise of eternal life with God.

Ponder: What is causing me great distress?

Prayer: Lord, your suffering and death gave us hope. Help me remain hopeful in the midst of personal struggles and worldly concerns.

Practice: Today I will be faithful by offering an encouraging word to someone in a distressful situation.

Tuesday of the Nineteenth Week in Ordinary Time

YEAR I
Deuteronomy 31:1–8
Deuteronomy 32:3–4, 7, 8, 9, 12

YEAR II
Ezekiel 2:8—3:4
Psalm 119:14, 24, 72, 103, 111, 131

YEARS I AND II
Matthew 18:1–5, 10, 12–14

[Jesus said], "Whoever becomes humble like this child is the greatest in the kingdom of heaven."

MATTHEW 18:4

Reflection: Humility is the quality of being teachable. Humility allows us to ask for help. Humility allows us to become vulnerable. Humility allows us to listen for God's voice. Humility allows us to acknowledge our dependence on God. Humility allows us to deepen our faith in God's care for us.

Humility allows us to be interested in others. Humility allows us to explore our inner lives to learn to be more like God in goodness, compassion, and love. Humility allows us to enjoy learning, expanding our horizons, and opening ourselves to endless possibilities for making positive change.

Pride and fear are the greatest barriers to a humble life. Pride is our smug assurance that we have all the answers, that our way of living is the right way, that the choices we make are better than the choices others make. Pride tells us we need not look at our flaws and weaknesses and that we need not feel compassion for those who need help.

Fear is an absence of love—love for ourselves, love for our neighbor, love for God. Fear is a reaction to hurt, rejection, abandonment, and physical, mental, emotional, and spiritual abuse. Out of fear, we close our hearts to love in the mistaken belief that we're protecting ourselves from further wounds.

Out of our desire to be more like Jesus, we can learn to humbly let go of pride, overcome fear, and be more childlike: Loving, vulnerable, dependent, curious, trusting, and willing to learn.

Ponder: How do I overcome pride and fear?

Prayer: Lord, you teach us by your loving and compassionate example. Grant me a humble heart, that I may always learn from you.

Practice: Today I will be faithful by acknowledging any mistake I make.

Wednesday of the Nineteenth Week in Ordinary Time

YEAR I

Deuteronomy 34:1–12
Psalm 66:1–3, 5, 8, 16–17

YEAR II

Ezekiel 9:1–7; 10:18–22
Psalm 113:1–2, 3–4, 5–6

YEARS I AND II

Matthew 18:15–20

[Jesus said], "For where two or three are gathered in my name, I am there among them."

MATTHEW 18:20

Reflection: God is always with us in our hearts and in all creation. Yet beyond our personal relationship with God, Jesus assures us that when we're in loving relationship with one or two or more people, he's there among us.

Being in loving relationship with others is one of our most difficult tasks. We struggle to accept others as they are without desiring or needing to change them, to let others be—perfectly and imperfectly—themselves. We're supposed to forgive others, yet we tend to hold on to resentment when others have treated us with unkindness, unfairness, or cruelty.

We remember Jesus told us to feed the hungry, clothe the naked, and visit the sick and imprisoned, yet our own needs tend to take priority over the needs of the poor and lonely. We have been taught that we're made in God's image of love and goodness, yet we often treat others with anger and hostility rather than with the compassion and peace of God.

As we live and work together, we can intentionally take a moment to stop and remember that where there is love, Jesus is among us. With that remembrance, we realize we have the power to choose love rather than anger or fear, compassion rather than judgment or disdain, and peace rather than conflict or aggression. We have the power to feel Jesus' presence by our faith in the power of love.

Ponder: How do I live and work with others?

Prayer: Lord, your love is a tangible presence among us. Keep me faithful to your command to love my neighbor as myself.

Practice: Today I will be faithful by sharing Jesus' love when I'm with others.

Thursday of the Nineteenth Week in Ordinary Time

YEAR I
Joshua 3:7–10, 11, 13–17
Psalm 114:1–2, 3–4, 5–6

YEAR II
Ezekiel 12:1–2
Psalm 78:56–57, 58–59, 61–62

YEARS I AND II
Matthew 18:21–19:1

"'Should you not have had mercy on your fellow-slave, as I had mercy on you?'"

MATTHEW 18:33

Reflection: When in doubt about how to treat others, we must look to Jesus. He shows us that we must be ready to offer a healing hand to those who ask our help, share a meal with social misfits, welcome outcasts into our midst, and be ready to serve the needs of the poor and ill.

Jesus shows us that we must teach God's love and compassion by *being* love and compassion in our human encounters and in our relationships with family, friends, neighbors, coworkers, and community members. He shows us that we must always forgive those who injure us, choose mercy over blame, and let go of desire for revenge, retaliation, or retribution.

God's Spirit in our hearts is forever pointing us to imitate the way of Jesus, yet sometimes we resist. We hang on to bitter feelings, we nurture grudges, and we foster animosity by keeping the memory of painful experiences alive. Yet we needn't hold on to anger, sadness, or resentment. With God's help, we can accept our difficult feelings and be willing to forgive those who have hurt us. With forgiveness comes a feeling of freedom and the energy to move on.

We have been given the power to love, heal, and show mercy. Our challenge is to intentionally choose to be like God, who loves us completely, forgives us without question, and calls us to an ever more compassionate way of being.

Ponder: When have I found it difficult to forgive?

Prayer: Lord, you love and forgive us even when we forget you. Open my heart to forgive those I resent.

Practice: Today I will be faithful by asking God to bless someone who has hurt me.

Friday of the Nineteenth Week in Ordinary Time

YEAR I
Joshua 24:1–13
Psalm 136:1–3, 16–18, 21–22, 24

YEAR II
Ezekiel 16:1–15, 60, 63
Isaiah 12:2–3, 4bcd, 5–6

YEARS I AND II
Matthew 19:3–12

[Jesus] said to them, "It was because you were so hard-hearted that Moses allowed you to divorce your wives, but at the beginning it was not so."

MATTHEW 19:8

Reflection: We all know people who have been divorced. We know the pain and betrayal of infidelity. We know the anger and blame that come from broken promises. We know the divisions and conflict that come from alienation. We know the sense of grief and failure that comes from lost relationships.

We also know that God loves us unconditionally and forgives our failures, weaknesses, betrayals, selfishness, and human inability to love as God loves. Whenever we worry about those who have experienced broken relationships, we can remember that God loves everyone without exception in this moment, in every moment. And we are called to do the same.

We can work on being compassionate and accepting in all situations. We can work on forgiving those who have hurt or betrayed us. We can work on increasing our generosity toward the poor and marginalized. We can work on improving our ability to respond with kindness and patience to those who are ill, complaining, or ungrateful.

Jesus tells us that the greatest commandment is to love God with all our heart, soul, strength, and mind—and that the second greatest is to love our neighbor as ourselves. When we are intentional about loving others, we're able to look past the surface of human flaws and weaknesses to see the embodiment of God's love and goodness. When we soften our hearts and let go of our tendency to judge, we become channels of God's pure and unconditional love.

Ponder: What relationships do I need to work on?

Prayer: Lord, you are our strength and courage. Show me how to be committed to your law of love.

Practice: Today I will be faithful by being more sensitive to those who are divorced or separated.

Saturday of the Nineteenth Week in Ordinary Time

YEAR I
Joshua 24:14–29
Psalm 16:1–2, 5, 7–8, 11

YEAR II
Ezekiel 18:1–10, 13b, 30–32
Psalm 51:12–13, 14–15, 18–19

YEARS I AND II
Matthew 19:13–15

Then little children were being brought to [Jesus] in order that he might lay his hands on them and pray.

MATTHEW 19:13A

Reflection: Children aren't small adults. They're complete people, but they don't think, act, or interact like adults. They need special care and attention at each phase of development. We must give our children age-appropriate tasks while guarding against overburdening them with adult responsibilities. We must show our children good eating habits, the importance of taking time for physical exercise, and the need for quiet hours of playing, reading, and being with God.

We must teach our children to be comfortable in the natural world. We must model positive dialogue and interesting conversational exchanges for our children. We must nurture our children's creativity. We must welcome our children's curiosity and see the world through their eyes of wonder. We must remember that children are a gift, not a burden, and that they depend on us for love, security, and hope.

Jesus reminds us that children have a special connection with God. Their innocence, vulnerability, openness, capacity for learning, and ability to live in the moment are qualities we must cherish and imitate. Our faith teaches us that we all—adults and children—are God's children, and we must be willing to let God guide us, comfort us, and show us how to live. God will never overwhelm us with responsibilities beyond our abilities. God delights in our curiosity and creativity, loves us unconditionally, welcomes our companionship in every moment, and never finds us burdensome.

Ponder: When do I need to be childlike?

Prayer: Lord, you welcome all children. Help me become more childlike in my love and dependence on you.

Practice: Today I will be faithful by supporting a child-protection program.

Twentieth Sunday
in Ordinary Time

YEAR A

Isaiah 56:1, 6–7
Psalm 67:2–3, 5, 6, 8
Romans 11:13–15, 29–32
Matthew 15:21–28

Jesus left that place and went away to the district of Tyre and Sidon. Just then a Canaanite woman from that region came out and started shouting, "Have mercy on me, Lord, Son of David; my daughter is tormented by a demon."

MATTHEW 15:21–22

Reflection: We care about our family, neighbors, and friends. We want them to have long, happy, healthy, and good lives. We stand by them when they're mentally, emotionally, spiritually, and physically impaired. We call a doctor when a family member becomes ill. We research community services for a neighbor struggling with addiction. We recommend professional counseling to a friend battling depression. We're able to find the best people and services to help the people we love get well.

We're blessed to have people who care for us when we're tormented by a debilitating condition. We must be aware that people throughout the world are being tormented by disease, malnutrition, dehydration, physical abuse, and oppression. They feel abandoned and have no access to doctors, community services, and counselors. Many people die before food, water, and other relief arrives.

People of faith understand that God's love and compassion transcend boundaries of race, gender, ethnic origin, social background, and religious tradition. We are called to be God's instruments of love and compassion to all people. We must pray for our abandoned, sick, and poor brothers and sisters. We must also work with other concerned groups and provide them with material resources to rebuild their lives, families, and communities.

Ponder: Who needs my care and attention at the moment?

Prayer: Lord, you offered the healing love and compassion of God to the sick and poor. Help me be an instrument of God's love and compassion to all people.

Practice: Today I will be faithful by visiting someone I've neglected.

YEAR B

Proverbs 9:1–6
Psalm 34:2–3, 4–5, 6–7
Ephesians 5:15–20
John 6:51–58

Be careful then how you live, not as unwise people but as wise, making the most of the time, because the days are evil. So do not be foolish, but understand what the will of the Lord is.

EPHESIANS 5:15–17

Reflection: We need order to limit chaos and avoid confusion. We post signs to guide us, warn us, and keep us safe. We must pay attention to the speed limits. We're conditioned to stop on red, slow down on yellow, and go on green. When we don't obey speed limits and traffic signals, accidents happen and people's lives are endangered. We have rules and laws to help keep civility in our society, to protect people's property, and to promote the common good. When people ignore the rules and disobey the laws, disorder and unrest result.

Life is good when we exercise self-control and set personal limits and attainable goals. We help keep order when we're careful to control our tongue, keep our hands to ourselves, and respect people's property, personal space, and privacy. People feel safe and secure in public places when we don't take advantage of the weak but are gentle and kind toward everyone.

People of faith are aware that a divine law is planted in our hearts. Our lives are formed and guided by God's wisdom, which teaches us the way of love, compassion, forgiveness, and peace. We are called to discern daily the wisdom of God and to align our thoughts and actions with the will of God. We strive always to reflect the wisdom of God in our environment and interaction with others.

Ponder: What do I need to be more careful about?

Prayer: Lord, you reveal the wisdom of God in the hearts of all people. Help me teach others by example the wisdom of your love, forgiveness, and peace.

Practice: Today I will be faithful by being more wise than foolish.

YEAR C
Jeremiah 38:4–6, 8–10
Psalm 40:2, 3, 4, 18
Hebrews 12:1–4
Luke 12:49–53

"I came to bring fire to the earth, and how I wish it were already kindled! I have a baptism with which to be baptized, and what stress I am under until it is completed! Do you think that I have come to bring peace to the earth? No, I tell you, but rather division!"

Luke 12:49–51

Reflection: We admire people who help the poor and homeless rebuild their lives. We marvel at the people who give up financial security and material comforts to do volunteer work with refugees in settlement camps in other parts of the world. We respect people who take care of abandoned children living with HIV/AIDS. We applaud those who courageously advocate for the protection of human life and the eradication of racism, discrimination, human trafficking, global poverty, violence, and war. We're in awe of countless people from diverse walks of life committed to doing good works for others.

People who have a deep passion to make a difference challenge us. We're forced by their life-witness of service to reexamine our mission and purpose.

We're deeply moved by their selfless acts of love and compassion. We're provoked to reassess our values, change our lifestyle, expand our worldview, rethink our positions on social issues, and work on our relationships.

People of faith realize that living the gospel isn't easy. We understand that taking a prophetic stance means speaking up for the poor and being on the side of love, forgiveness, nonviolence, and peace. We must pray to the Holy Spirit to kindle in us the fire of God's love and the courage to bring it to the earth now.

Ponder: What is my purpose?

Prayer: Lord, you send us your Spirit to renew the face of the earth. Filled with your love, help me make a difference.

Practice: Today I will be faithful by being true to my heart.

Monday of the Twentieth Week in Ordinary Time

YEAR I
Judges 2:11–19
Psalm 106:34–35, 36–37, 39–40, 43, 44

YEAR II
Ezekiel 24:15–23
Deuteronomy 32:18–19, 20, 21

YEARS I AND II
Matthew 19:16–22

[Jesus said to him,] "If you wish to enter into life, keep the commandments."...The young man said to him, "I have kept all these; what do I still lack?"

MATTHEW 19:17B, 20

Reflection: How many of us could face Jesus and say confidently that we've never killed, committed adultery, stolen, lied, or been disrespectful toward our father and mother?

Many of us have killed others' enthusiasm with our indifference or extinguished our own hopes by being afraid to take a chance. Many of us have been unfaithful to others when we gossip or reveal private matters. Many of us have taken items that don't belong to us from hotels or our workplaces. Many of us have lied to save face, cover transgressions, or protect ourselves. Many of us have been rude to our parents, treated them with scorn, or ignored them when they were old and in need of our care.

At the heart of all of God's commandments is love. When we wonder if we're faithful keepers of the commandments, we need to ask ourselves: Are we loving others as God loves us? Are we free of resentment, prejudice, and fear in our dealings with others? Are we serving the needs of those less fortunate? Are we patient with those who have difficult personalities? Do we share our resources as generously as possible? Do we approach life with a humble reliance on God's guidance?

As we learn to be more like Jesus, we grow in our ability to love as Jesus loves. As we practice loving others unconditionally, we'll be able to tell Jesus with true humility that we've done our best to keep God's commandments.

Ponder: Which commandment is most difficult for me to keep?

Prayer: Lord, you are the way to eternal life. Help me grow like you in love and service.

Practice: Today I will be faithful by choosing one commandment to reflect on and practice with love.

Tuesday of the Twentieth Week in Ordinary Time

YEAR I
Judges 6:11–24
Psalm 85:9, 11–12, 13–14

YEAR II
Ezekiel 28:1–10
Deuteronomy 32:26–27, 27cd–28, 30, 35cd–36ab

YEARS I AND II
Matthew 19:23–30

Then Jesus said to his disciples, "Truly I tell you, it will be hard for a rich person to enter the kingdom of heaven. Again I tell you, it is easier for a camel to go through the eye of a needle than for someone who is rich to enter the kingdom of God."

MATTHEW 19:23–24

Reflection: We live to be happy and prosperous. We consider ourselves rich if we have good health, an education, a job, a home, a car, financial security, a supportive family, loving friends, and other resources to have a comfortable lifestyle. When we step back and look at our lives, we see that we have many blessings. At times, we take our blessings for granted, but we appreciate the material things we've worked for. We value our relationships.

We know how quickly we can lose the things we possess. Along life's journey, we may experience hardships that destabilize our lives and family. We can get sick. We can find ourselves in financial trouble, lose our job, our home, and all the comforts of life. In a short period, we can become poor and be forced to rely on others. Our material possessions don't guarantee security and happiness.

People of faith trust in the providence of God. We know that everything, including the kingdom of heaven, is a gift from God. We're called to be predisposed to show compassion to others, live in moderation, and share what we have with anyone in need. The good life is measured not by what we possess but by the way we love God and our neighbor.

Ponder: What do I need to lead a good life?

Prayer: Lord, you give those who trust in you the gift of eternal life. Help me trust in you and live with simplicity of heart.

Practice: Today I will be faithful by donating some of my material possessions to charity.

Wednesday of the Twentieth Week in Ordinary Time

YEAR I
Judges 9:6–15
Psalm 21:2–3, 4–5, 6–7

YEAR II
Ezekiel 34:1–11
Psalm 23:1–3a, 3b–4, 5, 6

YEARS I AND II
Matthew 20:1–6

[Jesus said to them,] "For the kingdom of heaven is like a landowner who went out early in the morning to hire laborers for his vineyard."

MATTHEW 20:1

Reflection: The kingdom of heaven is like the landowner in that God keeps reaching out to people everywhere, inviting us to be part of God's work of love. The kingdom of heaven is like the landowner in that God welcomes all people from every walk of life into the kingdom. The kingdom of heaven is like the landowner in that God treats everyone equally, loving us all unconditionally, forgiving us with infinite mercy, walking with us in compassion and faithfulness all the days of our lives.

In the kingdom of heaven there is always unending love—however late in the day we show up. In the kingdom of heaven, our wages are love, and everyone receives the same wage of infinite love from God.

Love never ends. When we extend ourselves to show kindness, to thank someone for kindness toward us, to listen to someone's troubles, or to trust someone with our concerns, we multiply the love in the world. When we rejoice in others' happiness, encourage those who feel they've failed, spend time with someone lonely, or invite someone to have a meal, we multiply the love in the world.

We have no need to hold on to love or to be jealous, envious, or fearful that there isn't enough love to go around. Love never runs out; love never diminishes. When we love generously, love expands exponentially. When we let go of wanting something in return for our love, we are truly in the kingdom of God.

Ponder: How much love am I willing to share?

Prayer: Lord, you are my shepherd. Teach me to share your love with everyone.

Practice: Today I will be faithful by being intentional about loving my neighbors.

Thursday of the Twentieth Week in Ordinary Time

YEAR I
Judges 11:29–39
Psalm 40:5, 7–8, 8–9, 10

YEAR II
Ezekiel 36:23–28
Psalm 51:12–13, 14–15, 18–19

YEARS I AND II
Matthew 22:1–14

"The kingdom of heaven may be compared to a king who gave a wedding banquet for his son. He sent his slaves to call those who had been invited to the wedding banquet, but they would not come."

MATTHEW 22:2–3

Reflection: We love celebrations and parties. We take delight in planning events for family, neighbors, colleagues, and special friends. We spend a great deal of time scrutinizing the guest list before sending out invitations. We invite people we know and cherish.

We're honored when we're invited to a family gathering, birthday party, wedding ceremony, baby shower, or retirement party. Receiving an invitation means we hold a special place in the hosts' hearts.

We show respect and gratitude by accepting the invitation and showing up.

We may not respond so quickly to an invitation to volunteer at a soup kitchen, help build a house for a homeless family, or join the board of directors of an organization for victims of domestic violence. We may deliberately ignore invitations to attend meetings to address global poverty, drug abuse, and human trafficking. We may decline invitations to attend interreligious events that promote respect and universal peace.

People of faith respond to invitations to be in communion with God. We welcome invitations to join Bible-study groups and prayerfully reflect on the Word of God. We don't ignore the open invitation to worship, and we give thanks to God at the Eucharist, celebrate the sacrament of reconciliation, and serve the community.

Ponder: How do I respond to God's invitation of friendship?

Prayer: Lord, you invite us to be with you in the kingdom of heaven. Open my heart to accept your offer of forgiveness and peace.

Practice: Today I will be faithful by reexamining my relationship with God.

Friday of the Twentieth Week in Ordinary Time

YEAR I
Ruth 1:1, 3–6, 14–16, 22
Psalm 146:5–6, 7, 8–9, 9–10

YEAR II
Ezekiel 37:1–14
Psalm 107:2–3, 4–5, 6–7, 8–9

YEARS I AND II
Matthew 22:34–40

"Teacher, which commandment in the law is the greatest?" [Jesus] said to him, "'You shall love the Lord your God with all your heart, and with all your soul, and with all your mind.' This is the greatest and first commandment. And a second is like it: 'You shall love your neighbor as yourself.'"

MATTHEW 22:36–39

Reflection: When we wonder how to do God's will, the answer is simple: *Love.* Love God. Love self. Love neighbor. When we expend our energy on the work of love, we obey the will of God.

Love is practicing patience, generosity, and forgiveness. Love is showing compassion to people who are suffering. Love is being the peacemaker, rejecting violence and seeking to collaborate.

Love is choosing respectful words. Love is treating everyone with courtesy. Love is sincerely welcoming people we don't know, people we dislike, and people we fear. Love is overcoming prejudice. Love is accepting our differences. Love is honoring our common humanity, our common dignity, and our common heritage as children of God.

Love is giving up our comfort to support someone in need. Love is sharing our food and clothing with those who have none. Love is offering shelter to the homeless. Love is showing up in times of trouble. Love is making time for personal interactions. Love is taking an interest in others.

Love is spending time with God. Love is reading sacred Scripture. Love is listening to the silence of our hearts.

Love is actively looking to find God in every person—including ourselves—so we remember that God surrounds us and is the source of the love we pour out.

Ponder: How do I practice the two great commandments of love?

Prayer: Lord, you made us for love. Open my mind, soul, and heart to love you and my sisters and brothers.

Practice: Today I will be faithful by intentionally practicing love.

Saturday of the Twentieth Week in Ordinary Time

YEAR I
Ruth 2:1–3, 8–11; 4:13–17
Psalm 128:1–2, 3, 4, 5

YEAR II
Ezekiel 43:1–7ab
Psalm 85:9ab and 10, 11–12, 13–14

YEARS I AND II
Matthew 23:1–12

[Jesus said,] "Nor are you to be called instructors, for you have one instructor, the Messiah."

MATTHEW 23:10

Reflection: Jesus the Messiah, the Christ, is our instructor. He's the only teacher we need as we join to make God's vision of love, compassion, peace, and unity a reality. He's the only teacher we need to deepen our faith in our own goodness and in the goodness of all God's children.

Jesus, our teacher, shows us how to love one another by serving others' needs. He teaches us to touch others' lives with healing, compassion, and comfort. He teaches us to answer when someone calls for help. He teaches us to make room in our homes and hearts for people who aren't welcome elsewhere. He teaches us to forgive people who hurt us.

Jesus, our teacher, shows us how to be in relationship with God by going to a quiet place to pray. He teaches us to call God our Father. He teaches us to confide our fears and worries to God. He teaches us to retreat from the busyness of life to be refreshed by intimate moments with God. He teaches us to call out to God when we're suffering and in pain. He teaches us to seek the will of God and carry it out to the best of our ability. He teaches us to have faith in God's love and care for us.

Jesus, our teacher, shows us how to deepen our likeness to God's goodness and love by living simply without being attached to material possessions. He teaches us to walk humbly, to love deeply, and to serve God in whatever way God calls us.

Ponder: What has my faith taught me about Jesus?

Prayer: Lord, you are kindness and truth, justice and peace, love and compassion. Teach me your ways.

Practice: Today I will be faithful by asking Jesus to be my teacher.

Twenty-first Sunday in Ordinary Time

YEAR A

Isaiah 22:19–23
Psalm 138:1–2, 2–3, 6, 8
Romans 11:33–36
Matthew 16:13–20

"I will give you the keys of the kingdom of heaven, and whatever you bind on earth will be bound in heaven, and whatever you loose on earth will be loosed in heaven."

MATTHEW 16:19

Reflection: We have keys to our home, car, office, storage room, safe-deposit box, locker, and other important areas. We know the keys can't open and close on their own; the person with the keys is the controlling agent. We're responsible for the keys and must use them with awareness. We don't want the keys to be lost or to fall into the wrong hands, lest all our possessions and valuables be taken. We discern whether a person is trustworthy before handing over our keys.

We have other keys—freedom, knowledge, wisdom, love, compassion, forgiveness, and peace. We know these keys have no power to do anything on their own.

We must discern how, when, and where to use these keys. We can use these keys to open our minds and hearts to the beauty of creation, life, and humanity. We can use these keys to liberate people from oppression, illiteracy, ignorance, hatred, suffering, conflict, and violence. We must be careful not to lose these keys or have them taken away against our will.

People of faith understand that we've been entrusted with the keys to the kingdom of heaven. We've been given access to God's love, compassion, forgiveness, and peace. Under the guidance of the Holy Spirit and the wisdom of the community, we carry out God's mission by spreading the Good News of the kingdom to people everywhere.

Ponder: Do I take responsibility for my actions?

Prayer: Lord, you entrusted the keys of the kingdom of heaven to your people. Help me be your wise and responsible servant.

Practice: Today I will be faithful by being more aware of my personal responsibilities.

YEAR B

Joshua 24:1–2a, 15–17, 18b
Psalm 34:2–3, 16–17, 18–19, 20–21
Ephesians 5:21–32
John 6:60–69

So Jesus asked the twelve, "Do you also wish to go away?" Simon Peter answered him, "Lord, to whom can we go? You have the words of eternal life. We have come to believe and know that you are the Holy One of God."

JOHN 6:67–69

Reflection: Our words reveal who we are. Our words give people hints about our innermost thoughts, our worldview, perception of others, priorities, personal values, and principles. We use words to build committed, trusting, loyal relationships.

Our actions also reveal who we are. Our actions connect us to people's lives, create human experiences, and stimulate a variety of responses. Our actions reflect a lifestyle that gives people a sense of our life's direction. People come to believe and know us by our words and actions.

Our words and actions can cause difficulty in our relationships when they don't nourish goodness, life, love, intimacy, understanding, forgiveness, and peace. Our words and actions become a destructive force in the community when they intimidate the weak and promote misunderstanding, hatred of others, conflict, division, abuse, and violence. Our words and actions can manipulate minds and hearts, keep them in the dark, and deprive them of freedom. We must be aware of how our words and actions build or destroy life and relationships.

People of faith trust the life-giving words and actions of God in Jesus. Our lives are nourished by the Word of God and Jesus' teachings. Our words and actions flow out of our life with Jesus. Our direction is always a movement toward Jesus, who is the way, the truth, and the life. We're called to make the words and actions of Jesus our own, leading others to the gift of eternal life.

Ponder: What do my words and actions say about me?

Prayer: Lord, you have the words of eternal life. Help me believe and trust in the power of your Word.

Practice: Today I will be faithful by sharing this meditation with a friend.

YEAR C

Isaiah 66:18–21
Psalm 117:1, 2
Hebrews 12:5–7, 11–13
Luke 13:22–30

Someone asked [Jesus], "Lord, will only a few be saved?" He said to them, "Strive to enter through the narrow door; for many, I tell you, will try to enter and will not be able."

LUKE 13:23–24

Reflection: We long to belong. We strive to find our place. We work hard to be noticed and accepted. We struggle to join the latest fad. We want to join an elite club, to be part of the in-crowd action and excitement. We want to be constantly connected to something greater than ourselves. We feel safe and secure within our group of special friends.

We have a different perspective when we're turned down, turned away, denied, disconnected, pushed out, pushed back, pushed aside, ostracized, or rejected. We don't like being excluded from the family, the community, the group, the team, the club, or the chatroom.

Yet we live in a world where many people are excluded from their communities because of their race, language, gender, ethnic background, social status, and way of life. Some people believe certain other people have no dignity and no right to be members of the human family.

People of faith know God's kingdom is a gift. God's universal plan includes people from the east, west, north, and south. Our vision of life must be a reflection of God's will. We're called to love God and our neighbors. Our mission on earth is to welcome and accept all persons as sons and daughters of God.

Ponder: Whom do I exclude from my life and inner circle?

Prayer: Lord, you came to offer the gift of salvation to all people. Help me embrace all people with a loving and compassionate heart.

Practice: Today I will be faithful by being nonjudgmental and accepting.

Monday of the Twenty-first Week in Ordinary Time

YEAR I
1 Thessalonians 1:2–5, 8–10
Psalm 149:1–2, 3–4, 5–6, 9

YEAR II
2 Thessalonians 1:1–5, 11–12
Psalm 96:1–2a, 2b–3, 4–5

YEARS I AND II
Matthew 23:13–22

[Jesus said,] "Woe to you, blind guides, who say, 'Whoever swears by the sanctuary is bound by nothing, but whoever swears by the gold of the sanctuary is bound by the oath.' You blind fools! For which is greater, the gold or the sanctuary that has made the gold sacred?"

MATTHEW 23:16–17

Reflection: We must always be looking beyond the surface, beyond the glitter, beyond the success symbols, beyond the personality quirks to find the mystery of our true nature. We must never mistake the outer appearance, worldly possessions, social status, nationality, race, culture, or way of life for the real mystery of who we are. Each of us is a sanctuary for

God's Spirit. Each of us is a holy place where God's Spirit dwells. Each of us is a temple of the divine.

When we glimpse the sacredness of each human life, we begin to walk with greater reverence in others' presence. We begin to speak more kindly and respectfully. We begin to feel the awesome power of God's presence in ourselves and in others. We become humbled with wonder and gratitude that God has made us to carry God's holy presence.

To live each day with the consciousness of the mystery of God—in us, around us, in everyone we encounter—is to be blessed with a vision of the kingdom of God. Our eyes are opened to our magnificence and our fragility. We understand the need for great faith, patience, love, compassion, forgiveness, and mercy in our relationships, for we are all one in the mystery, one in our sacredness, one in God.

Ponder: When have I encountered the mystery of God's presence in others?

Prayer: Lord, you love your people. Heal my blindness, that I may see your holy presence in everyone.

Practice: Today I will be faithful by treating everyone with reverence.

Tuesday of the Twenty-first Week in Ordinary Time

YEAR I
1 Thessalonians 2:1–8
Psalm 139:1–3, 4–6

YEAR II
2 Thessalonians 2:1–3a, 14–17
Psalm 96:10, 11–12, 13

YEARS I AND II
Matthew 23:23–26

[Jesus said,] "Woe to you, scribes and Pharisees, hypocrites! For you tithe mint, dill, and cummin, and have neglected the weightier matters of the law: justice and mercy and faith."

MATTHEW 23:23

Reflection: Jesus tells us to stop focusing on relatively unimportant things and instead use our energy to practice justice, mercy, and faith.

We practice justice by being honest in our dealings with others. We avoid lies, cover-ups, and deception. We practice justice by being people of integrity. We are faithful to our commitments, trustworthy and dependable. We practice justice by treating all people equally. We accept and welcome others regardless of race, culture, ethnicity, social status, or way of life.

We practice mercy by forgiving those who have hurt us. We let go of resentment and desire for revenge. We practice mercy by forgiving ourselves for the pain we've inflicted on others. We take responsibility for our words and actions and make amends wherever possible. We practice mercy by letting our compassion touch others. We bring our healing presence to people who are ill, lonely, dying, or suffering.

We practice faith by surrendering our lives and our will to God's tender care. We pray for knowledge of God's will for us and the grace to carry it out. We seek to know God more intimately by studying sacred Scripture and meditating on God's Word manifested in Jesus.

We have been given a precious lifetime to reveal justice, mercy, and faith. We learn to carry the weight of this spiritual practice lightly by yoking ourselves to Jesus.

Ponder: How do I practice justice, mercy, and faith?

Prayer: Lord, you have searched me and you know me. Help me give more weight to matters of the Spirit. Help me grow in love and compassion.

Practice: Today I will be faithful by finding opportunities to practice justice, mercy, and faith.

Wednesday of the Twenty-first Week in Ordinary Time

YEAR I
1 Thessalonians 2:9–13
Psalm 139:7–8, 9–10, 11–12

YEAR II
2 Thessalonians 3:6–10, 16–18
Psalm 128:1–2, 4–5

YEARS I AND II
Matthew 23:27–32

"Woe to you, scribes and Pharisees, hypocrites! For you are like whitewashed tombs, which on the outside look beautiful, but inside they are full of the bones of the dead and of all kinds of filth. So you also on the outside look righteous to others, but inside you are full of hypocrisy and lawlessness."

MATTHEW 23:27

Reflection: We work hard to keep a good appearance in the presence of others. We want our life to appear to be nearly perfect. We want to come from a wonderful family. We want to have a beautiful house, a stylish car, a prominent position, and recognition in the community so our public image will appear flawless. We exude a sense of self-confidence by exaggerating our credentials, skills, and accomplishments. We want to be held in high regard so we can have power and influence over others.

Our public persona often hides our inner reality. We pretend our life is perfect, but we come from a dysfunctional home. We pretend to be self-confident, but we feel abandoned and lack self-worth. We pretend to be a caring person, but we have no capacity to show love and compassion. We pretend to have influence and power, but we're paralyzed by fear. We pretend to enjoy life, but we're filled with pain and sadness. We pretend to be at peace, but we're mentally and emotionally distressed. We pretend to be all-knowing, but we're lost and confused.

People of faith must avoid being hypocrites and live in the light of the gospel. Our words and actions must not betray God's will, which is planted in our hearts. We are called to be the image and likeness of God.

Ponder: What am I pretending to be?

Prayer: Lord, you created us in your image and likeness. Help me be an authentic witness of your love and compassion.

Practice: Today I will be faithful by avoiding hypocrisy.

Thursday of the Twenty-first Week in Ordinary Time

YEAR I
1 Thessalonians 3:7–13
Psalm 90:3–4, 12–13, 14, 17

YEAR II
1 Corinthians 1:1–9
Psalm 145:2–3, 4–5, 6–7

YEARS I AND II
Matthew 24:42–51

[Jesus answered them,] "Therefore you also must be ready, for the Son of Man is coming at an unexpected hour."

MATTHEW 24:44

Reflection: Imagine yelling at someone, complaining, lying, stealing, gossiping, giving someone the cold shoulder, treating someone with contempt, cheating on a test—and having Jesus walk in. Immediately we would be conscious that we'd failed to practice God's commandment to love our neighbor as ourselves. We'd be aware that we had failed ourselves, for we are all made in the image of God's love and goodness.

We all have the power of patience, compassion, forgiveness, acceptance, and love. We all have the ability to choose our way of being in the world.

When we fail to choose loving words, actions, and behaviors, we fail to serve one another with compassion, respect, and mercy—to love our neighbors as ourselves—as Jesus called us to do. Our faith tells us that God is ever present to us, that God's Spirit is in our hearts, that whenever two or more are gathered in Jesus' name, he is also there. This means the Lord is always walking into our lives. The Lord is in every moment and every breath. Every second of our day is an encounter with the Lord. We're meeting the Lord everywhere, in every relationship, in every person.

The time to choose love, compassion, respect, mercy, forgiveness, peace, reconciliation, and unity is now. Now is the moment of our encounter with the Lord. Now is the coming of the Son of Man.

Ponder: How do I put into practice what I believe?

Prayer: Lord, you are always with me. Help me stay awake and alert to your presence, that I may choose love, compassion, and peace in my interactions.

Practice: Today I will be faithful by choosing words and actions that reveal God's love.

Friday of the Twenty-first Week in Ordinary Time

YEAR I
1 Thessalonians 4:1–8
Psalm 97:1, 2, 5–6, 10, 11–12

YEAR II
1 Corinthians 1:17–25
Psalm 33:1–2, 4–5, 10, 11

YEARS I AND II
Matthew 25:1–13

"The foolish said to the wise, 'Give us some of your oil, for our lamps are going out.' But the wise replied, 'No! there will not be enough for you and for us; you had better go to the dealers and buy some for yourselves.'"

MATTHEW 25:8–9

Reflection: Christians are called to give food to the hungry, drink to the thirsty, and homes to the homeless. We're called to forgive, love our enemies, and love our neighbors as ourselves. All the service we give, all the generosity we show, and all the kindness and encouragement we pour out is our humble effort to be like Jesus. When we feel impatience, frustration, annoyance, and dislike, we struggle to turn those negative feelings into patience, acceptance, forgiveness, and compassion. This is our daily call, our daily task, our daily privilege.

This inner spiritual work is our own; we can't do it for anyone else. We can show others a way of being that reflects the love of God, but we can't control how others react to us or how they lead their lives.

Like the wise bridesmaids, we intentionally choose to keep an extra supply of love and faith at hand by praying, meditating, and spending quiet time with God. Like the bridesmaids, we keep our lamps ready to shine with our inner goodness and love so we're always ready to see the face of God in others.

Ponder: Where do I go when my love and compassion are depleted?

Prayer: Lord, thank you for your love and guidance. Help me keep a healthy supply of love in my heart so I can respond generously to my sisters' and brothers' needs.

Practice: Today I will be faithful by taking five minutes alone with God to replenish my reserves of love and serenity.

Saturday of the Twenty-first Week in Ordinary Time

YEAR I
1 Thessalonians 4:9–12
Psalm 98:1, 7–8, 9

YEAR II
1 Corinthians 1:26–31
Psalm 33:12–13, 18–19, 20–21

YEARS I AND II
Matthew 25:14–30

"His master said to him, 'Well done, good and trustworthy slave; you have been trustworthy in a few things, I will put you in charge of many things; enter into the joy of your master.'"

MATTHEW 25:21

Reflection: The love of God has been handed to us to put to good use in our troubled world. Are we willing to take a risk to love and be loved? Are we willing to be God's trusted servants in the work of love? Are we afraid of love?

Each evening, it's helpful to look back over the day and consider our words, actions, and behaviors to discern habits and attitudes that may help or hinder our ability to relate to others in a loving and harmonious manner.

How did we use our gifts and talents to help others? How did we show love? Did we ignore an opportunity to help? Were we indifferent to someone who needed us? Did we stay in touch with God? Did we ask God to show us what to do and how to do it? Were we inspired by the Holy Spirit?

With the gift of each new day come many opportunities to develop our talents, use our creativity, and make a positive impact. Each day, we have the choice to multiply our love and compassion by facing the world with a smile, looking for the good in everyone we meet, and practicing gratitude for all we've been given.

Ponder: How am I a trusted servant of God?

Prayer: Lord, you have entrusted your love to us. Release me from the bonds of fear, that I may love my neighbor as myself.

Practice: Today I will be faithful by taking a few minutes to examine my day and see where I loved, where I failed to love, and where God guided me.

Twenty-second Sunday in Ordinary Time

YEAR A

Jeremiah 20:7–9
Psalm 63:2, 3–4, 5–6, 8–9
Romans 12:1–2
Matthew 16:21–27

> But [Jesus] turned and said to Peter, "Get behind me, Satan! You are a stumbling block to me; for you are setting your mind not on divine things but on human things."
>
> **MATTHEW 16:23**

Reflection: The path to a good, happy, prosperous, and successful life isn't easy. We're often distracted by personal and worldly matters. We experience a mixed bag of success and failure, happiness and disappointment, order and chaos. We do our best to work through the challenges, remove the stumbling blocks, and overcome the temptations. We're not always successful, but we struggle to move forward.

One of the most difficult challenges is learning the art of self-acceptance. We listen to faulty messages that say we're not good enough. We deny our innate beauty and goodness. We're blind to our unique gifts and talents. We allow fear and self-hatred to become stumbling blocks to our personal growth and development. We're tempted to give up, act irresponsibly, and blame others for our unhappiness. We can't progress until we believe in our own goodness, put fear and self-hatred behind us, and overcome the temptation to make others our scapegoat.

People of faith set our minds and hearts on divine things, not on human things. We believe God has a plan. We're given the grace of discernment and the strength to do God's work on earth. We have confidence as sons and daughters of God that, with the help of the Spirit, we'll remove the stumbling blocks and overcome temptations that prevent us from spreading the Good News.

Ponder: What are my challenges, stumbling blocks, and temptations?

Prayer: Lord, your resurrection conquered sin and death. Give me the strength to overcome pride so I can become a humble servant of your love and peace.

Practice: Today I will be faithful by honestly naming and facing my stumbling blocks.

YEAR B

Deuteronomy 4:1–2, 6–8
Psalm 15:2–3, 3–4, 4–5
James 1:17–18, 21b–22, 27
Mark 7:1–8, 14–15, 21–23

"For it is from within, from the human heart, that evil intentions come."

MARK 7:21A

Reflection: We know that everything in the world has an origin. We may have an interest in the origin of the universe, earth, water, life, and human civilization. We may be curious to find the origin of our name. We may be fascinated with the origin of music and words. We may want to know the origin of a food, spice, plant, animal, or piece of jewelry. We have a richer understanding of something when we know its origin.

The human heart is a metaphor for the human person. We need to pay more attention to our heart, which is the interior origin of our intentions. We express ourselves in the world through our words and actions. We need to be more self-aware before we speak and act. We need to make sure that our intentions reflect the type of person we want to be before we manifest ourselves to others.

Our words and actions reflect what is in our heart. They have the potential to build or destroy life, human relationships, and communities. When we align our intentions with goodness, love, compassion, forgiveness, and peace, we can become what we intend. People will have a deeper understanding of our heart by our words and actions.

People of faith are encouraged to reflect on God's Word as the source and foundation of the moral life. We use the Ten Commandments as guidelines for living in right relationship with God and neighbor. We purify our heart's intentions with prayer and fasting. Life is good when our thoughts and actions reflect God's will.

Ponder: What is in my heart?

Prayer: Lord, you come from the heart of the Trinity. Give me a pure heart, that I may reflect goodness and love.

Practice: Today I will be faithful by examining my heart before I speak and act.

YEAR C

Sirach 3:17–18, 20, 28–29
Psalm 68:4–5, 6–7, 10–11
Hebrews 12:18–19, 22–24a
Luke 14:1, 7–14

"For all who exalt themselves will be humbled, and those who humble themselves will be exalted."

LUKE 14:11

Reflection: We enjoy being the center of attention. We talk about ourselves, our interests, our problems, our work, and all we've accomplished. We drive a nice car, dine at fine restaurants, and wear expensive clothes. We associate with people of prominence, influence, and power. We intimidate, criticize, and mock others to make ourselves look good. We like being in control and having power over others. We feel good when people honor us, raise us up, and promote our causes. We're happy as long as things go our way.

But life is out of balance when we're the main attraction. We must be aware of others' concerns and be a willing listener. We must simplify our lives and help the poor. We must walk in solidarity with the powerless and become advocates of nonviolence, justice, and peace. We must be gentle, loving, compassionate, and welcoming toward all people regardless of race, color, gender, nationality, religious tradition, and social condition. We must honor, defend, and lift up the oppressed. We feel more fulfilled when we're selfless rather than self-serving.

As people of faith, we choose to imitate the humble life of Jesus—who came to serve, not to be served. We have concern for others and offer assistance to those in need—not to be rewarded, but to fulfill the command to love our neighbor. We take the humble approach to life, recognizing the truth that God's love shows no partiality.

Ponder: What lifestyle changes do I need to make?

Prayer: Lord, you came to be the humble Servant of God to all people. Give me a humble heart so I may be a selfless, compassionate servant to the poor and vulnerable.

Practice: Today I will be faithful by quietly reaching out to anyone in need.

Monday of the Twenty-second Week in Ordinary Time

YEAR I
1 Thessalonians 4:13–18
Psalm 96:1, 3, 4–5, 11–12, 13

YEAR II
1 Corinthians 2:1–5
Psalm 119:97, 98, 99, 100, 101, 102

YEARS I AND II
Luke 4:16–30

[Jesus] unrolled the scroll and found the place where it was written: "The Spirit of the Lord is upon me, because he has anointed me to bring good news to the poor."

LUKE 4:17B–18A

Reflection: By our baptism, we've been anointed to bring Good News to the poor. God's Spirit is upon us and within us to guide us as we answer this call to share God's love every day, especially with the poor.

Many kinds of poverty exist. With material poverty, people have no food to eat, no clothes to wear, no water to drink, and no access to education. By comparison, we lead lives of plenty and even luxury. The good news we can bring to the materially poor is our willingness to share from our abundance, to work on being more generous, and to let go of selfishness, negative judgment, and indifference.

With emotional poverty, people have shut themselves off from love, compassion, and kindness. Out of fear of being vulnerable, their hearts remain closed. The good news we can bring to the emotionally poor is our willingness to love unconditionally, to accept others as they are, and to be emotionally stable and trustworthy so others feel safe in our presence.

With spiritual poverty, people have lost faith in God's presence, goodness, and love. The good news we can bring to the spiritually poor is our faith. Each day we can ask God to show us what to do. We can spend time reading Scripture, praying, and meditating. We can put our trust in God and let go of our need to control people, events, and things.

Ponder: What good news do I bring to the poor?

Prayer: Lord, your love and goodness fill the world. Open my eyes, ears, and heart to your presence in the poor.

Practice: Today I will be faithful by giving from my abundance to help the poor.

Tuesday of the Twenty-second Week in Ordinary Time

YEAR I
1 Thessalonians 5:1–6, 9–11
Psalm 27:1, 4, 13–14

YEAR II
1 Corinthians 2:10b–16
Psalm 145:8–9, 10–11, 12–13ab, 13cd–14

YEARS I AND II
Luke 4:31–37

[Jesus] went down to Capernaum, a city in Galilee, and was teaching them on the sabbath. They were astounded at his teaching, because he spoke with authority.

LUKE 4:31–32

Reflection: We need to cultivate habits that keep us healthy. We cultivate the habit of grooming our bodies to be clean. We cultivate the habit of eating natural foods to strengthen our immune system. We cultivate the habit of reading to enlighten our minds. We cultivate the habit of working to become mature and responsible. We cultivate the habit of physical exercise to stay fit.

We must cultivate practices that sustain community life and our interpersonal relationships. We must cultivate gratitude. Recognizing and appreciating our blessings and others' gifts and talents prevent us from hurting people.

We must cultivate the practice of telling the truth. When we keep our word and honor our commitments and promises, we build trust and confidence in our relationships, community, and workplace.

We must cultivate the practice of hospitality. Inviting others to be with us and live with us affords us opportunities for sharing and mutual learning. Welcoming people from diverse backgrounds dispels fear of strangers.

People of faith cultivate spiritual practices to deepen our relationship with God and neighbor. We cultivate the practices of prayer, fasting, and almsgiving to live spiritually. We read and meditate on the Word of God to enlighten our minds and nourish our hearts. We honor the Lord's Day and keep it holy. We fulfill God's mission in the world by embracing the life, teachings, and ministry of Jesus.

Ponder: What habits, practices, and rituals sustain my life?

Prayer: Lord, you teach us how to live a holy life. Help me be more disciplined in showing love, compassion, and forgiveness.

Practice: Today I will be faithful by praying, fasting, and giving alms to the poor.

Wednesday of the Twenty-second Week in Ordinary Time

YEAR I
Colossians 1:1–8
Psalm 52:10, 11

YEAR II
1 Corinthians 3:1–9
Psalm 33:12–13, 14–15, 20–21

YEARS I AND II
Luke 4:38–44

Now Simon's mother-in-law was suffering from a high fever, and they asked [Jesus] about her. Then he stood over her and rebuked the fever, and it left her.

LUKE 4:38B–39A

Reflection: In times of illness, we are blessed when family, friends, and neighbors care about us and look after us. We're fortunate when others advocate for us and make sure we're getting the right medical attention. We're enriched by prayers others offer on our behalf. Sometimes we're called to pray for others, and we do so out of love and compassion.

When a serious illness reverses itself, we hope our intercessory prayer has prompted a miracle. Sometimes our prayers for a cure go unanswered, however, and we're left wondering why God doesn't always answer as we'd like. This is when we most need faith. We must trust that God cares. We must trust that God heals in every dimension, not just the physical dimension. We must trust that what God does in our lives makes sense, even if we don't understand it.

Our faith has its foundation in the resurrection of Jesus, who proves that death has no power over us. Death is a transformative event both for the one who dies and for those of us who grieve the loss of a loved one's human presence. When we live by faith, we accept that our human vision is limited. In humility and trust, we place our lives and our will into the care of God, who loves us without end.

Ponder: When have I experienced God's healing?

Prayer: Lord, your love and goodness touch my life. Help me trust your kindness and accept your peace.

Practice: Today I will be faithful by being more trusting and less controlling.

Thursday of the Twenty-second Week in Ordinary Time

YEAR I
Colossians 1:9–14
Psalm 98:2–3, 3–4, 5–6

YEAR II
1 Corinthians 3:18–23
Psalm 24:1bc–2, 3–4ab, 5–6

YEARS I AND II
Luke 5:1–11

Then Jesus said to Simon, "Do not be afraid; from now on you will be catching people." When they had brought their boats to shore, they left everything and followed him.

LUKE 5:10B–11

Reflection: We like stability. We have a routine. We order the same thing for breakfast and the same thing for lunch. We go to and from work the same way. We follow the same schedule. We keep company with the same group of friends. We shop at the same stores. We complain about the same things over and over again. We practice the same habits. We hold on to them for personal safety and security.

We become unsettled when people and situations challenge us to change. Seeing a homeless person on the street challenges us to sacrifice our breakfast or lunch. Listening to a parent who lost a child challenges us to change our outlook on life. Watching an undocumented immigrant be harassed challenges us to change the way we approach strangers. Hearing about the millions of starving people challenges us to talk to our friends about doing something to eradicate global poverty. Sitting next to someone of a different race and culture challenges us to look at our prejudices.

People of faith listen attentively to God's Word. We allow God's Word to touch our hearts and change our lives. We forfeit the safe routines of life and embrace the mysterious call to follow in the footsteps of Christ. Our true vocation is to become coworkers of Christ, bringing the healing love and compassion of God to all people.

Ponder: Who makes me feel unsettled?

Prayer: Lord, you call us to leave everything and follow you. Help me detach from the securities of life and trust in doing your work of healing and reconciliation in the world.

Practice: Today I will be faithful by letting go and letting God lead me.

Friday of the Twenty-second Week in Ordinary Time

YEAR I
Colossians 1:15–20
Psalm 100:1, 2, 3, 4, 5

YEAR II
1 Corinthians 4:1–5
Psalm 37:3–4, 5–6, 27–28, 39–40

YEARS I AND II
Luke 5:33–39

"And no one after drinking old wine desires new wine, but says, 'The old is good.'"

LUKE 5:39

Reflection: We tend to be afraid of change. We like places, people, and ideas to be familiar and comfortable. We resist challenges to our way of life, our way of thinking, our routines, and our habits. Yet the nature of life is constant change. At the cellular level, our bodies are disintegrating, rebuilding, being transformed. At the emotional level, we fluctuate from sad to angry to happy to anxious to serene. At the mental level, our thoughts bounce from one topic to another. At the spiritual level, we play tug of war with God: Sometimes we let God direct us; sometimes we try to control people, events, and outcomes; sometimes we have faith in God's love; and sometimes we feel God has abandoned us.

When change comes from outside, we sometimes have the option to reject it and continue life as we are accustomed. Yet when we welcome change, we open ourselves to new adventures, new skills, new knowledge, and new people.

Sometimes we feel that a change is being imposed on us. We have the right to discern whether this change will help us deepen our capacity for love and compassion, open our hearts to know God more intimately, and help us stay faithful to our commitments to family, friends, and community.

Jesus invites us to let go of old, rigid thinking and fear and instead embrace the transforming power of God's love and compassion.

Ponder: What changes do I resist?

Prayer: Lord, you made us and we are yours. Take away my fear of change, that I may be transformed into a more perfect likeness of your love and goodness.

Practice: Today I will be faithful by letting go of an old habit that is no longer useful.

Saturday of the Twenty-second Week in Ordinary Time

YEAR I

Colossians 1:21–23
Psalm 54:3–4, 6, 8

YEAR II

1 Corinthians 4:6b–15
Psalm 145:17–18, 19–20, 21

YEARS I AND II

Luke 6:1–5

Then [Jesus] said to them, "The Son of Man is lord of the sabbath."

LUKE 6:5

Reflection: It makes good sense for us to take one day a week to rest from work and give our attention to God in thanksgiving. Yet nowadays we're as busy on Sunday as we are the other days of the week. We shop for the week's food, catch up on the week's laundry, clean house, make household repairs, and prepare and freeze meals for the week ahead. We take trips, go to the mall, pay our bills, and tackle our homework.

Although we might rebel against a law that makes us take an enforced day of rest, we need to take a deeper look at the spirit of the command to keep holy the Sabbath. God cares about us. God knows we can't keep up a frantic pace without mental, physical, emotional, and spiritual harm. God invites us to slow down, take a break from worldly concerns, and focus on the things of God: peace, harmony, serenity, joy, love, and compassion. We need time to incorporate the things of God into our hearts and minds. We need time to enjoy the gift of creation and our friends and families. We need time to relax and enjoy the sensation of being alive.

Whenever we feel life is getting too frantic, we can put on a Sabbath attitude: Take a break, take a breath, and know that God is near.

Ponder: How do I keep holy the Sabbath?

Prayer: Lord, you are lord even of the Sabbath. Help me make every day holy by taking time to be aware of your presence in the natural world, in my heart, and in others.

Practice: Today I will be faithful by taking an intentional Sabbath moment to rest, clear my thoughts, and thank God for my life.